AF552814

Scottsdale
Jewel in the Desert

Marjorie Thomas' oil painting titled Indian Ponies Going to Water *is from the collection of Mrs. Gene Brown Pennington.*

Scottsdale: Jewel in the Desert

An Illustrated History by Patricia Myers McElfresh

To Bill and Marge Weishaar,
may you enjoy "a trip back in time"
within these pages — as much as
your visit here with Bongaart.

Patricia Myers
March 31, 1989

"PARTNERS IN PROGRESS" BY LOIS McFARLAND

Sponsored by the
Scottsdale Historical Society

Windsor Publications, Inc.
Woodland Hills, California

IN LOVING MEMORY OF MY
MOTHER, ELIZABETH MYERS
SEITTERS, AND FATHER,
LAMOINE B. SEITTERS, AND
MY GRANDMOTHER, MYRTLE
L. SEITTERS, WHO GAVE ME
THE PRICELESS GIFTS OF
ENTHUSIASM, CONFIDENCE,
AND DETERMINATION

Windsor Publications, Inc.—History Books Division
Publisher: John M. Phillips
Staff for *Scottsdale: Jewel in the Desert*
Editor/Picture Editor: Teri Davis Greenberg
Editorial Director, Corporate Biographies: Karen Story
Design Director: Alexander D'Anca
Assistant Director, Corporate Biographies: Phyllis Gray
Editor, Corporate Biographies: Judy Hunter
Editorial Assistants: Patricia Buzard, Lonnie Pham, Pat Pittman
Production Artist: Beth Bowman
Marketing Director: Ellen Kettenbeil
Sales Manager: Ernie Fredette
Sales Coordinator: Joan Baker

Library of Congress Cataloging in Publication Data

McElfresh, Patricia Myers, 1933–
Scottsdale, jewel in the desert.

Bibliography: p. 127
Includes index.
1. Scottsdale (Ariz.)—History. 2. Scottsdale (Ariz.)
—Description. 3. Scottsdale (Ariz.)—Industries.
I. McFarland, Lois. Partners in progress. 1984.
II. Scottsdale Historical Society. III. Title.
F819.S37M34 1984 979.1'73 84–19605
ISBN 0–89781–105–4

Published 1984
Printed in the United States of America
First Edition

CONTENTS

Foreword 6

Preface 8

Acknowledgments 10

CHAPTER ONE
Roots of an Oasis 13

CHAPTER TWO
From Boom to Bust 23

CHAPTER THREE
Evolution of an Arts Colony 41

CHAPTER FOUR
Tourists and Townies 57

CHAPTER FIVE
Jewel in the Desert 71

CHAPTER SIX
Coming of Age in a New Age 85

CHAPTER SEVEN
Partners in Progress 99
by Lois McFarland

Patrons 126

Selected Bibliography 127

Index 128

FOREWORD

Will Rogers used to say, "The Indians never got lost because they were always looking back over their shoulders to see where they'd been." And so it is with Scottsdale today, looking back to see where we've been and how far we've come.

Someone recently wrote, "when an Easterner thinks of Arizona today, three things come to mind—the Grand Canyon, beautiful sunsets, and Scottsdale chic." Many Arizonans perceive Scottsdale as the place to move after one has made it financially. The opulent resorts that have sprung up in and around Scottsdale rank among the best in the world. Tourists who visit the Valley of the Sun don't consider their trips complete until they have visited the erstwhile "West's Most Western Town."

But it wasn't always this way. Scottsdale's meteoric rise to find its own place in the sun is relatively recent. Before World War II it was a quiet, close-knit farming community "way out east" of the hustle and bustle of Phoenix. The founding families sought to keep Scottsdale free of the moral decadence that so often accompanied new towns, and they succeeded. Growth was slow, but her citizens were of strong moral fiber. They were the quiet, hard-working, unheralded men and women who have gone largely unnoticed in the chronicles of Arizona's wild and woolly history.

In 1926, when my father, Ira "Happy" Trimble, moved across the Salt River with his family from Tempe, Scottsdale was still a farming community. Like many others, the Trimbles were health-seekers. My grandmother was so stricken with asthma that doctors in Texas gave her only a short time to live. That was in 1916. By the time they moved to Scottsdale 10 years later, she was working in the cotton fields and reputed to be one of the fastest pickers in the county. For a time she also ran a small restaurant on Brown Avenue that served home-cooked meals. She thrived in the Arizona sun and lived until the 1960s.

The year of the nation's bicentennial marked the 50th year of my father's arrival in Scottsdale. He was only a boy of 18 at the time, working long hours in the fields picking cotton to help support a large family. Despite his relative youth, his memory of Scottsdale during the 1920s was near-photographic. The town at that time consisted of a few adobe or frame houses shrouded by tall, stately trees stretched along dirt roads. Surrounding the tiny hamlet were fields of citrus, alfalfa, and cotton. Electric wires had been strung out from Phoenix only six years earlier. I have many happy memories of driving up and down the streets of modern-day Scottsdale with Dad describing in great detail where each farmhouse stood and reciting the names of the families who lived in them.

I still get those melancholy "Scottsdale blues" when I see new buildings going up and another piece of the desert being eaten up by creeping suburbia. But of all the cities in the Salt River Valley (and I've lived in most of them), Scottsdale is unique. When the population explosion caused other cities in the valley to expand unharnessed and out of control, Scottsdale maintained a policy of growth with planning and dignity. The result may not be 100 percent perfect, but all one has to do is look around.

Just about the time I get to thinking the town just "ain't" like it used to be, and it seems like everybody just moved here yesterday, I run into Thelma Steiner Holveck or Lester and Labeula Steiner Mowry. Those spunky Steiner girls were born here about the time Arizona became a state, and Lester moved here from Texas with his family in 1917. There are others too—the Hydukes, Corrals, Mildred Sullivan Eitel, and Earl Shipp. Each is a living link to Scottsdale's historic past. It is comforting to know they are still around, a reminder of those times of not so long ago.

Thanks to the wonderful work of Pat McElfresh, we have our history written down while folks are still around to tell it like it was. Like the Indians of whom Will Rogers spoke so eloquently, we too can look back over our shoulders to see where we've been.

Marshall Trimble
Director of Southwest Studies
Maricopa County Community College District

PREFACE

Scottsdale, a city whose roots are rural and religious, has evolved during the past century into a swank and sunny city of arts, entertainment, and easy-going charm. It has traversed far, evolving from a pastoral colony to a movie-set Western town and then into its modern image as a shimmering oasis for leisure and the arts.

It was a fascinating challenge to be chosen to write the narrative of this journey. During my research, I recognized from the start that Scottsdale had been imprinted by a special breed of people, people who were enthusiastic about their community, conscientious about its development, and proud of the result. I came to admire the city's founder, Chaplain Winfield Scott, a man eager for challenge throughout his life who, at the age of 51, founded a town that within a half-century would be on the brink of becoming one of the West's most vital cities and a magnet for people seeking a new life-style in the Southwest.

The book's title resulted from brainstorming telephone sessions with my editor, Teri Davis Greenberg. A jewel has many facets, and so does Scottsdale—business, family, leisure, arts, culture, and agriculture. This community was in its rough and unpolished gem stage when it was known as the "West's Most Western Town." But as it tumbled through the years, it gained a special sheen and developed into a city that radiates an image of the sophisticated new West while retaining the heritage of its roots.

As Scottsdale was taking root, the Santa Fe Railroad had arrived in Phoenix, boosting that 3,000-population town's bustling development. Mesa, to the southeast, had been founded by Mormons in 1878 and was both an agricultural and commercial center; Tempe to the south was the home of the Hayden Flour Mill and Tempe Normal School, drawing students, educators, and farmers to the town; Fort McDowell, a frontier Army outpost, had been established first in 1865 to the northeast, its duty to protect travelers and settlers from marauding Apache Indians. And then came Scottsdale, established by Army Chaplain Winfield Scott (a distant relative of General Winfield Scott of Mexican War fame).

It's no wonder that people always have been attracted here—it is magnetic country. The townsite of 1888 was nestled among several low mountain ranges: imposing salmon-hued Camelback Mountain on the west, Papago and Barnes buttes strangely rounded on the south, Mummy and McDowell mountains to the north, and the majestic Superstition Mountains and Four Peaks to the east. At daybreak and sundown the sun casts ever-changing shadows of purple, magenta, ochre, and bronze along the slopes. The pioneers surely must have sensed the power of the Southwest desert, as do those of us now living here.

Scottsdale has become a dynamic community with the attractive dual advantages of a sophisticated city bordered by open spaces. Residents today are committed to excellence in city government and the arts. They like living in this city, but they know there are problems, among them a lack of extensive public transportation, very little low-income housing, and not enough major corporations to expand in-town employment opportunities. Municipal issues are the same as in many growing cities: high-rise construction, traffic patterns, and residential services.

During my period of research and writing, I met many wonderfully interesting and kind people. In the first six months, I collected so much information that it overflowed filing cabinets in both my home office and a temporary one at the public library. At one point, I found myself involved in a sort of giant jigsaw puzzle. Richard Lynch's excellent biography of Chaplain Winfield Scott provided documented information about the town's development up to the founder's death in 1910. But data available about the years that followed was less systemized or readily available. It became my task to study and sort while pursuing further research through interviews, telephoning, and tracking down photographs.

Then came the difficult part: distilling the data into a readable, popular history of this city. I heard more tales than there was space to recount and, if I have any regrets, it is that there was not enough time to speak individually with many of my sources, and that much of our communication had to be by telephone or mail.

This print-portrait of the personality of a city is based on material collected by the city, colored by personal experiences of longtime residents, and flavored by memories. It makes no claim to be a definitive work, but it is hoped that this overview will provide an understanding and appreciation of what preceded for this generation of residents and those who will follow.

Patricia Myers McElfresh

ACKNOWLEDGMENTS

Many people have left their marks on this book by helping me locate information and photographs, and for being so generous in time, support, and encouragement. First and foremost is Thelma Steiner Holveck, who shared her personal treasury of Scottsdale historical materials, suggested sources, and shared her never-flagging enthusiasm. And likewise her sister, Labeula Steiner Mowry, and her husband, Lester Mowry, who loaned priceless photographs and kept a spirit-boosting attitude.

Many other residents were willing to take the time to answer questions, clarify information, or search for old photos. They include Alice Cavalliere, Alvaro Corral, Rachel Ellis, Barbara Ferris, Bill Kimsey, Paul Messinger, Joe Miller, Buck Saunders, Jean Thomas Scott, Wes Segner, Earl Shipp, Henry and Barbara Wick, Malcolm White, and many more.

Scottsdale Historical Society officers and members provided special help, among them President Don Prior, Curator Midge Roberts and past president William Jenkins. Without the Society's willingness to endorse this book, it would not have been published.

The materials amassed for the City of Scottsdale by Richard Lynch, author of the biography of Chaplain Winfield Scott, were used as the nucleus of my research, and I appreciate having access to those materials. The city staff, especially Mayor Herb Drinkwater, was helpful, including Library Director Linda Saferite, who graciously permitted a corner of the Southwest Room to be set aside as a depository for the city's historical materials and my temporary base of operations.

I am especially grateful to the Scottsdale Daily Progress: to publisher Jonathan Marshall for permission to use the newspaper's computerized word-processing system at night and on weekends, to production manager Jerry Ziegler for his skill and patience, and especially to the managing editor, my husband, Jerry McElfresh, for access to the newsroom's files and for providing invaluable information and insight based on his 20 years with the Progress.

Many of the photographs collected for the book would not have been available except for the generosity of Leonard Yuschik, Bob Petley, and Tom Johnson. I also am appreciative of the efforts of the Scottsdale Chamber of Commerce staff, and Carefree

Advertising's Jim Flynn and Dave Knox for providing information and photographs, and to Ted Hill Photography for prompt and high-quality reprint service.

Very special appreciation of his creativity is directed to free-lance photographer Rick Mueller, who delivered assignments of superb quality, always meeting deadlines. I am grateful to Lois McFarland for her careful work and warm writing for the Partners in Progress chapter.

The publishers, Windsor Publications, and staff members were infinitely patient and understanding, especially my editor, Teri Davis Greenberg. Her professional guidance, editing skills, continuous encouragement, ready ear, and consummate patience were remarkable, especially since both of us were experiencing births during this period—she as the mother of a baby girl and myself with the spawning of my first book.

Patricia Myers McElfresh

A 1906 or 1907 Thanksgiving dinner was given at Scott's ranch for residents and guests, many of whom were from the staff of the Elliott Sanatarium in Phoenix. Courtesy, Mrs. Ruth M. Elliott

CHAPTER ONE

Roots of an Oasis

The desert north of Scottsdale in 1983 appeared much as the land did to Chaplain Winfield Scott when he arrived nearly 100 years earlier—sun-parched, with only scrub vegetation, and the mountains in the distance. But he envisioned an oasis springing from the land, where people would live and enjoy the clean air and spacious surroundings. His vision came to be, and with it came the city now famed for its residential comfort and cultural ambience. Photo by Rick Mueller

The year was 1888. A bearded man sat on horseback, gazing across the central Arizona desert. He looked at the barren, sun-parched land and imagined an oasis that could nurture a new community. The man was U.S. Army Chaplain Winfield Scott, a Baptist minister who had been raised in western New York farming country who dreamed of a flourishing town site in the desert and then worked to turn that dream into reality. The result was the city that eventually bore his name—Scottsdale, Arizona.

Scott, the fourth of ten children, was born in a log cabin in West Novi, Michigan. He was college-educated, a devout minister, and a dedicated educator who became an innovative farmer, a progressive politician (serving in the territorial house of representatives in 1898 and supporting the concept of women's suffrage), and an always-enthusiastic promoter of the Salt River Valley, and especially of his own town.

That town took root in mid-February of 1888 when the 51-year-old chaplain, assigned to an Army post on Angel Island in San Francisco Bay, accepted an invitation to visit the Phoenix area, which then had a population of about 3,000. Civic and business leaders involved in the Arizona Improvement Company had contacted Scott and suggested that he check the development potential of the Salt River Valley. Although Scott was known to be a promoter of immigration, he came, in his own written words, "full of doubts . . . skepticism and prejudice." He stayed a week and, as he rode horseback around the east end of the valley, he liked what he saw and decided it would be his retirement base.

Scott was familiar with the irrigated citrus orchards of Southern California and recognized the land's potential. Five months after first coming to the valley, he proved his enthusiasm by arranging to pay two dollars and fifty cents an acre for a 640-acre section. Section 23, the nucleus of Scottsdale, is bounded today on the west by Scottsdale Road, on the south by Indian School Road, on the east by Hayden Road, and on the north by Chaparral Road.

On July 2, 1888, Scott made a down payment of $320 through an agent at the U.S. land office in Tucson. His claim was filed under the Desert Land Act of 1877, which required that land grants be irrigated within three years. He had no qualms about being able to irrigate the arid terrain. William J. Murphy, a New York contractor,

Opposite page
Captain Winfield Scott (far left), who was severely injured while serving in the New York Volunteer Infantry during the Civil War, remained an active farmer, rancher, minister, and traveler despite lifelong complications and pain. He was promoted to the rank of major following his retirement from the Army. Scott's wife, Helen Louise Brown Scott, is pictured at left. Courtesy, Interlaken Historical Society

Bottom
George Washington Scott, Winfield Scott's brother, was Scottsdale's first citizen-in-residence and worked with Pima Indians from the nearby reservation to clear away brush, plant crops, and dig irrigation ditches. Courtesy, Mrs. Lena Scott Polglase/City of Scottsdale

Below
Winfield Scott made a down payment of $320 (50 cents an acre for 640 acres) for land that became the nucleus of modern-day Scottsdale. Courtesy, Scottsdale Historical Society

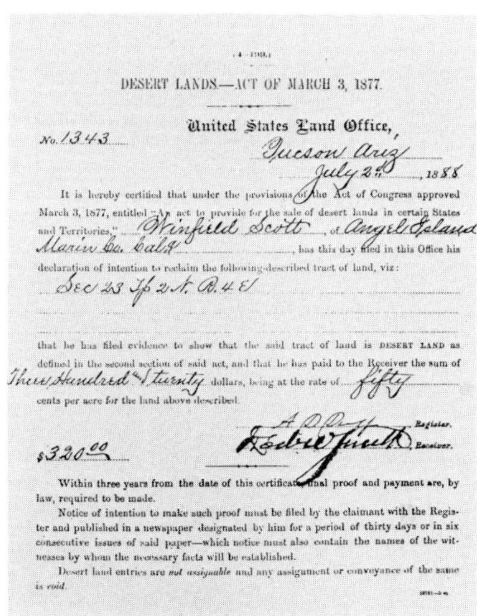

DESERT LANDS.—ACT OF MARCH 3, 1877.

United States Land Office,

No. 1343

Tucson Ariz

July 2nd, 1888

It is hereby certified that under the provisions of the Act of Congress approved March 3, 1877, entitled "An act to provide for the sale of desert lands in certain States and Territories," Winfield Scott, of Angel Island Marin Co. Cal. has this day filed in this Office his declaration of intention to reclaim the following-described tract of land, viz:

Sec 23 Tp 2 N. R. 4 E

that he has filed evidence to show that the said tract of land is DESERT LAND as defined in the second section of said act, and that he has paid to the Receiver the sum of Three Hundred & twenty dollars, being at the rate of fifty cents per acre for the land above described.

A. D. Duff, Register.
[illegible], Receiver.

$320.00

Within three years from the date of this certificate final proof and payment are, by law, required to be made.

Notice of intention to make such proof must be filed by the claimant with the Register and published in a newspaper designated by him for a period of thirty days or in six consecutive issues of said paper—which notice must also contain the names of the witnesses by whom the necessary facts will be established.

Desert land entries are *not assignable* and any assignment or conveyance of the same is *void*.

already had completed construction on the 35-mile-long Arizona Canal, which crossed the northwest corner of Scott's section, diverting river water to the area after rainfall. If Winfield Scott is to be designated as the father of Scottsdale, Murphy most certainly could be called the godfather.

But the father of Scottsdale was not the first resident of the future town. Because Scott still had Army obligations to fulfill, he asked his brother, George Washington Scott of San Francisco, to go to the area and start cultivation. George arrived in December 1888 to become Scottsdale's first citizen in residence. He cleared away greasewood growth, dug irrigation ditches, and planted crops. By February he had planted 80 acres of barley, a 20-acre vineyard, and a seven-acre citrus orchard. He probably was helped by Pima Indians hired from the nearby reservation.

Meanwhile, Winfield Scott spread the word about opportunities in Arizona during an assigned chaplain's tour of the Midwest. He said the area was as fertile as Egypt's famed Nile Valley, perfect for commercial fruit ventures, and more advantageous than California at market time because crops ripened a month earlier and the area was two days closer to eastern buyers.

After Scott was transferred in February 1889 to Fort Huachuca in southern Arizona, he attended to his developing ranch on furloughs, while also filling pulpits in Phoenix, Tempe, and Mesa.

Scott made his final land payment of $1,200 in September 1889 for a total of $1,520. A bit earlier he had sold 40 acres for $30 an acre to Mrs. Mary Brown White of Rochester, New York, probably to meet his payment. He also had to sustain the expense of water access. So in October 1889 he sold canal-builder Murphy 360 acres for $25 an acre. He returned title to the federal government for 40 acres located north of the Arizona Canal and of today's Camelback Road because they had not been irrigated. Scott retained 200 acres on which he grew citrus and other fruits, sweet potatoes, and peanuts.

In February 1894, a year after Scott retired from the Army and moved to his ranch, Rhode Island banker Albert G. Utley, who owned another section south of Scott's, announced plans to subdivide 40 acres into a town site by 1895. He put Scott in charge of the enterprise. Utley had bought the section for $1,000 in 1890 from his niece, Nannie C. Utley Fulwiler. (Her mother was Mrs. Leander Utley, the former Margaret Murphy, sister of canal king W.J. Murphy.)

Utley's plans included daily bus service to Phoenix, a sanatorium for respiratory patients, a complex of small homes to be rented to winter visitors, and a large resort hotel. Scott himself had plans to colonize an area north and east of the town site and to attract farmers to plant citrus trees and vineyards.

In 1894 the tiny desert colony was still a place without a name and had only a few residents living south of Scott's land. During his early development of the land, the chaplain was a good press agent for his work. He kept in contact with *The Phoenix Herald*, stopping by to tell the editors of his progress and often leaving a sack of sweet potatoes or a crate of raisins as proof. In early 1894 in a story announcing the newest phase of development, the *Herald* praised the innovative chaplain for his early successes in agricultural work, noting: "To his energy and devotion to the interests of that part of the valley is largely due the founding of this town."

Apparently the territorial press was influential in naming the chaplain's town. Some people had suggested that the area be named Murphyville in honor of the canal builder or Utleyville for the new developer. Utley, however, preferred the site to be called Orangedale because of the growing orange belt south of the canal along the length of Camelback Mountain's south face. But late in the summer of 1894 the name was changed from Orangedale to Scottsdale.

In the spring of 1895 *The Phoenix Herald* carried the first Scottsdale land advertisement, proclaiming in bold-face type: "Scottsdale Fruit Lands/New Town Just Starting." The ad told of the area's agricultural potential, about the many types of fruit already growing, and it promoted the chance to buy undeveloped land or near-mature orchards. There was even a quote from a physician stating that the location was ideal for health problems. The land was offered for $100 to $250 an acre—up to a 100 percent increase from Chaplain Scott's original cost.

Until 1895 only a few health-seekers and land speculators had shown interest in the area and had made their homes on the fringes of Scott's section. At that time it was said by local wags that the only reasons to live in Scottsdale were "busted health, busted wealth, or busted reputation." Most preferred the amenities available in Phoenix over the spartan, pioneer way of life in the desert to the east. But soon some people came to Scottsdale to enjoy the clean air, soft water, and fertile soil, while others came to experience a simple, wholesome way of life.

Of those who first came to join Scott, each brought his or her own particular visions and dreams to add to his. Many came hoping that the pure, clean, dry desert air would soothe lungs marred by tuberculosis, or relieve labored breathing caused by asthma and other respiratory ailments. Most of these settlers were cultured and nurtured the arts in this dusty little turn-of-the-century settlement.

Right
George Blount brought his wife Alza and three children to the desert for Alza's health, calling Scottsdale's environment "the cleanest, driest air" he could find. The Blounts were the first family, after Scott's, to settle in the townsite proper. Courtesy, Scottsdale Historical Society

Above right
Scott's Army mule, Old Maud, retired with the chaplain in 1893. Although Helen Scott is seated on the animal here, the children of the little town usually used the patient beast for rides. Courtesy, Mrs. Elsie Elliott Severance

Right
The Titus House, the oldest existing residence in Scottsdale, was built in territorial days in 1892. It has hardwood floors, 14-foot-high ceilings, and an Italian marble fireplace for one of its three chimneys. Courtesy, Scottsdale Daily Progress

J.L. Davis opened the first general store in Scottsdale at the southeast corner of Brown and Main. The building also housed the town's first post office, with Davis as postmaster. Courtesy, City of Scottsdale

Among these first arrivals were schoolteacher George Blount, his wife, Alza, and their three children. Earlier they had moved from Illinois to Phoenix for Mrs. Blount's health. In 1895 Blount bought 40 acres in Scottsdale to gain access to what he considered "the cleanest, driest air" in the area. Thus, his family was the first to settle in the community after the Scotts. The Blounts' adobe home, erected just south of the corner of what is now Civic Center Plaza and Second Street, held the first school classes, which were taught by Mrs. Blount.

From Missouri came Wilford and Mittie Hayden (for whom Hayden Road was named), who first lived near Phoenix until the flood of 1891 ruined their farm. They moved to higher ground two miles southeast of Scott's ranch, and their six children helped the community reach the number required to form School District 48. It was designated in the summer of 1896 as "Scotts-Dale," and was the first official recognition of the town.

In true western tradition the men assembled one Saturday morning to raise a one-room schoolhouse while the women prepared a picnic meal in Scott's shady grove. The next day a Sunday School was organized in the 16-by-18-foot room, and services were held. Mrs. Blount, the first teacher, was paid $40 a month when school opened September 28, 1896, with 14 pupils for the eight-month term. The wooden school was used for 13 years before a new school was built.

The Scottsdale community grew as people from surrounding areas moved in. They included the families of Thomas U.Z. King, John S. Tait, and Frank F. Titus. Titus, a railway executive, built an impressive brick home in 1892. It is still inhabitated at 1310 N. Hayden Road, south of McDowell Road, and is listed in the National Register of Historic Places. Titus reportedly built what became known as "The Mansion of Arizona" to house important eastern visitors he brought in from the railhead at Prescott, then the territorial capital.

Young Verner A. Vanderhoof, who had come from Kansas for health reasons, found the Titus ranch when he desperately needed work. He toiled for a summer as a citrus day laborer, living in a crude tent on the mansion's grounds. He later entered college, became a teacher, a rancher (with Scott's help and encouragement), and then a minister in the community. On August 2, 1900, his daughter, Perla May, was the first Anglo child born in Scottsdale and lived there all her life.

Scottsdale was put on the map in August 1897 with its first post office, which was run by J.L. Davis. The previous May Davis had opened the first general store at the southwest corner of Brown and Main. Davis' store spared residents long trips by horse or wagon to Tempe or Phoenix for shopping. Despite this convenience, most supplies remained scarce.

At this time most of Scottsdale's residents still lived in primitive tent-houses—wood-framed structures with white canvas that could be rolled up and down to let in the breeze on summer nights or keep out the cold in winter. Inside these dwellings were, perhaps, a few basic pieces of furniture brought from the East or Midwest with orange crates serving as shelves. This housing gave rise to the town's unattractive nickname, "White City."

Living in this tent city were a number of ministers and their families, and soon Scottsdale, with a population of 60 or 65, was becoming known as a closely knit, generally well-educated Christian community. This group of clergymen was responsible for keeping the community dedicated to temperance. Utley's lot, which had been designated for the store and post office, had a deed restriction prohibiting the sale of intoxicants. The town had the first Anti-Saloon League in the territory, and in May 1897 Scottsdale voted for prohibition. That was when Alza Blount was quoted in *The Phoenix Herald* as saying, "It is the determination of the first settlers in Scottsdale never to let alcohol get a foothold in this part of the valley."

These first highly religious settlers also showed a strong sensitivity for their Indian neighbors. When Scott first bought his land, he went to the Pima chief and asked permission to settle there. He later preached Christianity to the Indians and created a cemetery for them. In return the Pimas taught Scott and other early residents how to build *ramadas*—brush shade arbors of cottonwood branches—outside the tent homes. Throughout the ensuing years both Pimas and Apaches came to town in their wagons on weekends, quietly offering baskets, pottery, and firewood for sale, and enjoying a bottle of soda pop before going back to the reservation.

The Indians also came to love and respect Minnie Elliott, who came from Kansas City, Missouri, with her husband, the Reverend Judson A. Elliott, and their three children. Mrs. Elliott, a victim of tuberculosis, had been told she had six months to live and had decided to make her last weeks count. So she went to the reservation to teach the Indians hygiene and nutrition. The Indians, in return, worked to restore her health. They had her lie in the warm sand under mesquite trees and gave her herb teas. Within six months her lungs had cleared, and she lived to be 82 years old.

The 1897 contingent also included Howard and Ida Underhill, who had come from New York because of Mrs. Underhill's ill health. They first lived in a tent-house and later built a large

Opposite page, top
The Scottsdale community was closely knit, with members often going for outings such as picnics at Hole-in-the-Rock at Papago Park. Families would bring fresh fruits or preserved foods to share, spread a cloth on the ground, and gather next to it on blankets. Courtesy, Scottsdale Historical Society

Bottom
The Underhill home was the site in 1903 for the wedding of two new residents, Walter P. Smith and Helen Greene (center). Helen and Chaplain Scott are fourth and fifth from the left; Ida and Howard Underhill are second and third from left. Verner Vanderhoof is the tall man, fourth from the right. The little girl in front is May Vanderhoof, his daughter. Courtesy, Mrs. May Vanderhoof Mathis

impressive home with a wide veranda near the northwest corner of present-day Scottsdale and Indian School roads. They purposely built the house extra-large and were the first Scottsdale residents to offer their home to paying winter visitors.

The Arizona Investment and Land Company, organized in 1885 by Murphy and several investors, began advertising the availability of Scottsdale land at $100 an acre for 250-acre parcels. The ads touted, "Where the soil is the most fertile in the world, where five acres will make a man independent, and the person with small capital can get a start." Even this enticement apparently did little for the development of the community, which slowed around 1897 by a period of drought that lasted until the great floods of 1905.

At the turn of the century, the Thomas family of Illinois came to Scottsdale for father Stanley's health. Son George was born in March 1901 in a small brick house on the corner of what is now Indian School Road and Brown Avenue. He is recorded as the first Anglo male born in the town site. His father died in 1902, and his mother Sarah supported her three children by taking in laundry and baking bread for the general store. She was the town's first postmistress from April 5, 1904, to April 22, 1913.

Town father Scott traveled in the Southwest, Midwest, and East for both clerical and mining interests. When back on his ranch, Scott continued to be active in dairy and alfalfa farming into his seventies.

Then three tragic events marred Scott's retirement years: a fire in 1895 that destroyed most of the family's possessions; the extended drought that ruined most of his citrus orchards; and a murder that took place in 1901 on the Scott ranch. A man known as "Popcorn John" Rubenstein (because he sold popcorn on the Phoenix courthouse plaza) carried the daily mail and habitually had lunch on Scott's property before returning to the city. One day a wagon blocked his way and he inexplicably shot two of the field hands. One was a Pima Indian, so Scott, despite having been bedridden because of a broken leg, drove his carriage to the Pima village to inform the chief and to assure him that a Scottsdale resident was not involved.

Scott, who meanwhile had received a post-retirement military promotion to the rank of major, still traveled frequently but came back often for brief visits. He and his wife returned permanently in 1905. On October 19, 1910, at the age of 73, Scottsdale's founder died of complications following abdominal surgery.

About the time of the chaplain's death many of Scottsdale's old guard settlers left the area, the Elliotts, Blounts, Underhills, and Davises included among them, and a new wave of residents arrived to continue the town's development.

SCOTTSDALE

100 LOTS AT AUCTION

Thursday, Jan. 22nd

10:30 A. M. TO 3 P. M.

AT SCOTTSDALE

The Pasadena of Arizona

Big Free Cafeteria Lunch At Noon

FREE TRANSPORTATION

Automobiles will take all prospective buyers out, provided they register at

No. 129 N. First Ave. By Wednesday Night

TERMS:—Your only chance to buy a Business or Residence lot your own price and still on our easy terms—$10 down and $10 per month, or 5% discount for all cash.

COME! EVERYBODY HAS A GOOD TIME and makes easy money at Getsinger's auctions.

Arizona Investment & Land Co.

129-131 North First Avenue

B. W. GETSINGER, Auctioneer

16 East Adams Street

CHAPTER TWO

From Boom to Bust

The land boom was starting in Scottsdale in 1914, when this advertisement appeared in the Arizona Gazette *on January 19. The imaginative designer depicted a camel-accompanied desert dweller casting an eye on a verdant valley of lush crops growing next to the Arizona Canal. As an inducement to buy in "the Pasadena of Arizona," the advertisement promised automobile rides, a free lunch, and "everybody has a good time and makes easy money at Getsinger's auctions." Courtesy, Scottsdale Historical Society*

The development of central Arizona moved slowly through the years of drought and flood until progress began to be made in controlling the precious water that drained into the Salt River from mountains to the north and east. A long, low structure called Granite Reef Dam was built northeast of Scottsdale in 1908 by the Salt River Valley Water Users Association to divert the Salt River into its canal system. Water storage was provided upstream by the Roosevelt Dam, which was completed with federal assistance in 1911. Both dams helped to alleviate the floods that often followed droughts and to provide a more dependable water supply. However, there still were seasons when heavy rains filled the Indian Bend slough that ran southward through town into the Salt River and flooded ranches and made the dirt roads impassable along the way.

The reliable water supply opened a new era in the Salt River Valley. Scottsdale's real-estate values quadrupled because of growing interest in the area's healthy environment and new economic opportunities. These opportunities stimulated a major immigration of California families to Arizona.

In 1912 Jacob and Lorene Steiner moved from Santa Barbara. Two daughters, Thelma and Labeula, were born in Scottsdale. Thelma Steiner Holveck, who later became assistant city clerk, recalled that her mother, who was a nurse, worked with Dr. B.B. Moeur (who later became governor) and helped deliver many babies. One of these children was born to neighbors Laurie and Maggie Gammill, who named the infant Zona because she was born in 1914, two years after Arizona attained statehood.

Many others were attracted to Scottsdale, and land sales accelerated after an October 14, 1913, *Arizona Gazette* story detailed plans for 10,000 acres to be developed the following year. "An earthly paradise where every prospect pleases," touted the front-page headline. A headline below the first announced: "Scottsdale, lovely oasis where olives and fruit vie with cotton and alfalfa in paying tribute to soil of great richness."

Among those attracted to Scottsdale at the time was Charles Miller (for whom Miller Road was named). He had come to the valley in 1908, and in 1913 he bought 160 acres of Scott's original section for $75 an acre, four times the price of four years before.

Opposite page, top left
Jacob and Lorene Steiner moved to Scottsdale in 1912 from Santa Barbara, California, to operate a dairy and feed farm. Courtesy, Thelma Steiner Holveck/Labeula Steiner Mowry

Top right
Fruit trees flourished on the Jacob Steiner farm. Here Labeula and Thelma help their daddy select the best citrus. Courtesy, Thelma Steiner Holveck/Labeula Steiner Mowry

Bottom left
E.O. Brown practically owned the town. He was its storekeeper and then ran a cattle ranch and the community cotton gin. Brown Street was named for him. Courtesy, City of Scottsdale

Bottom right
Mrs. Arthur Crews, her children, and their friends pose in front of the Crews' home at the corner of Scottsdale Road and Main Street. Notice the canvas flaps in place of glass windows or screens. Courtesy, Emmajeane Harris

The chaplain's beloved olive trees had survived the drought years, and 10 acres still had thriving fruit trees from Scott's original groves.

Miller was followed by more families—Thomas, Brown, Coldwell, Graves, Crews, and Peterson among them. In 1909 Edwin O. Brown took over J.L. Davis' general store at the corner of Main Street and Brown Avenue, the street later named for the storekeeper. In subsequent years Brown also operated the community cotton gin, a cattle ranch north of town, and served as postmaster and as a school trustee. Thus he became one of the most influential members of the community.

At about this time, the valley's first resorts began to take root. The Ingleside Inn had been completed in 1909 just outside of Scottsdale at what is now 60th Street and Indian School Road. From the Midwest came Edward Graves, who bought the Oasis Villa (Underhill home) in 1910, renamed it Graves Guest Ranch, and catered to vacationers as well as tuberculosis patients. Graves also ran an Indian curio shop at the ranch and set up an Indian arts store in Phoenix in 1912. His wife, Mary, attended to the daily needs of guests. In Chandler, to the south, the impressive San Marcos Hotel opened in 1913. It helped to boost the valley's growing reputation as a resort area.

By now Scottsdale's population was nearing 200, but there wasn't one paved street in town. Modern-day Scottsdale Road started out as Murphy Avenue, and then was renamed Paradise Avenue because it led to the area to the north called Paradise Valley. Today's Indian School Road, which was Utley Avenue on the original town site map, was changed to Scott Avenue by 1913. Streets named Grant, Sherman, Sheridan, Garfield, and Ford later were changed to numbered streets and avenues. They remain so today.

The town began to attract renowned personalities. They included the Walthalls—actor Henry (internationally famous as the "Little Colonel" in D.W. Griffith's *Birth of a Nation,* as a cowboy film star, and as President Madero in *Viva Villa*) and his actress sister, Anna Mae. Both sought respite in Scottsdale from Hollywood's hectic pace. They visited their brother John at his territorial farmhouse at the southern edge of town.

Twenty-four-year-old artist Marjorie Thomas came in 1909 from New England for her mother's and brother's health. The Thomas family first homesteaded 160 acres of land at the foot of Mummy Mountain to the northwest, then built a studio at the corner of what are now Indian School Road and Civic Center Plaza.

In 1912 the St. Louis Writers Plantation Club was founded for writers and actors. It was built on 200 acres between Indian School

GRAVES RANCH

SCOTTSDALE

Convalesce Amid the Orange Groves on the Desert Edge---

HOME LIKE

Each patient at Graves Ranch is provided with a private cottage, clean and comfortable and furnished in a home like way.

All the comfort of a real home and in a climate that is with out a peer in the entire world.

Every chance in the world is thus given for a speedy recovery.

HOME COOKED MEALS

Everything that the market affords, and lots of it is one the table at Graves Ranch, and the finest home cooking you ever tasted, Special diets are provided for those who require them. All meals are a model of how good, clean food should be served.

EVERY CARE

is given that will add to the comfort of the patient.

Our patients are without a doubt the happiest, most contented you will ever see recovering health in one of the most beautiful spots in the world.

GRAVES RANCH

SCOTTSDALE, ARIZONA

MISS EMMA WOLF

Phone 126R12

Opposite page, left
The Graves Ranch, advertising in the Arizona Republican, *boasted of its private cottages for convalescents and its "home-cooked" meals that included special diets to aid in early recovery. Courtesy, City of Scottsdale*

Right, top
Poet Rose Trumbull wrote verse about life in the Old West. One of her poems, "The Breed of Men," challenged those raising cattle to pay heed to their children's needs for attention and guidance. Other poets who lived in Scottsdale in the early days included Jane P. Vanderhoof, Helen Scott, and, in later years, Patricia Benton. Courtesy, Scottsdale Historical Society

Right, bottom
Young Marjorie Thomas, who came to Scottsdale from New England in 1909 for her mother's and brother's health, became a popular artist. Courtesy, Thelma Steiner Holveck/Labeula Steiner Mowry

and Osborn roads near 64th Street, west of the canal.

Scottsdale also was discovered by tall, stately, white-haired Ohio artist Oscar Strobel, Jr., cowboy artist Lon Megargee, Eastern artist Jessie Benton Evans, and Oregon poet Rose Trumbull. As the years passed, more and more artists arrived, many of them excited about painting what they called "incomparable" desert scenery.

As the town's families grew, the little wooden one-room schoolhouse became inadequate, and a red brick structure was built in 1909 for a student body now numbering 32 pupils. Sand and gravel were brought by wagon from the Salt River bed, and bricks were hauled by wagon from Phoenix. The building cost $4,500 and provided two classrooms and a basement that was used as an auditorium. The Little Red Schoolhouse, as it became known, was dedicated on February 26, 1910. Among those at the dedication ceremony on Winfield Scott's 73rd birthday were Territorial Governor Richard Sloan and U.S. Vice President Thomas Riley Marshall, a part-time resident.

Vice President Marshall, who served two terms under President Woodrow Wilson, was married to the former Lois Kimsey. When in Scottsdale, the couple lived in a home on the south side of Indian School Road west of Scottsdale Road. They were more than seasonal visitors, however, becoming very much involved in community life. Mrs. Marshall's parents, William E. and Elizabeth Kimsey, who had been coming from Indiana during the winters since 1907 for Mrs. Kimsey's health, became year-round residents in 1915. Every winter Kimsey built another redwood house with a screened porch to rent or sell. Kimsey became the town's first justice of the peace, and a co-founder of Scottsdale's first bank and first power company, Scottsdale Light and Power Company.

In 1917 Kimsey's son, Mort, and Mort's wife, Clarice, moved to Scottsdale from the Midwest. Two years later Mort established the Scottsdale Service Company, a garage and service station at the northeast corner of Scottsdale and Main, which he ran until 1945. Mort, who later became the city's second mayor, was a favorite town figure, once described by a writer as "a tall, lanky cuss with graying brown hair and a droopy, Wyatt Earp mustache."

For decades the Little Red Schoolhouse served as the hub of community events—church services, public meetings, elections, dances, concerts, drama events, and May Day ceremonies. At Christmas the pupils decorated a palo verde tree or a cedar branch cut from Chaplain Scott's ranch with strands of popcorn and fresh cranberries.

Though the student body steadily grew in numbers, the Little Red Schoolhouse remained a one-teacher school that emphasized the three "R's" until 1912. Then domestic science classes were

SECURITY · ACRES

A subdivision of the W½ of NW¼ of NE¼, the NE¼ of SW¼ and the S½ of SW¼ of section 26, Township 2 North, Range 4 East, G.&S.R.B.&M., Maricopa County, Arizona.

Surveyed in April 1914 by Gus A. Streitz, C.E.

Scale: 1 inch = 500 feet.

SCOTTSDALE

Sec. 26

N.

11349
RECORDER'S OFFICE

DEC 14 1915

- DEDICATION -

The Arizona Securities and Investment Company by Ernest W. Lewis, its president, and Geo. A. Mintz, its secretary:

Do hereby publish this plat of Lots, Blocks, Streets and Alleys as the complete plan and survey of "Security Acres", being all of the W½ of NW¼ of NE¼, the NE¼ of SW¼, and the S½ of SW¼ of section 26, Township 2 North, Range 4 East, G. and S.R.B. and M., Maricopa County, Arizona; and the streets and alleys shown hereon are hereby dedicated to the use of the public as highways.

Arizona Securities and Investment Co.
by Ernest W. Lewis
President

[SEAL]

Geo. A. Mintz
Secretary

- ACKNOWLEDGEMENT -

State of Arizona }
County of Maricopa } ss

Before me George W. Elias a Notary Public in and for the County of Maricopa, State of Arizona, personally appeared The Arizona Securities and Investment Co. by Ernest W. Lewis, its president, and Geo. A. Mintz, its secretary, known to me to be the persons whose names are subscribed to the foregoing instrument and acknowledged to me that they executed the same for the purpose and consideration therein expressed.

Given under my hand and seal of office this 11th day of December, 1915.

George W. Elias
Notary Public

[SEAL]

My commission expires May 27, 1917

Opposite page, top
The Arizona Securities and Investment Company developed Security Acres, a 1,000-acre residential area, in 1914. Courtesy, City of Scottsdale

Bottom left
William E. and Elizabeth Kimsey came to Scottsdale in the winter of 1907. Later Kimsey became the town's first justice of the peace and founded the town's first bank and first power company. Courtesy, William L. Kimsey

Bottom right
Dora Jean Ellis (standing, left) was the first teacher in the Little Red Schoolhouse. In 1919, when this photo was taken, grades one through eight were taught in the same classroom. Courtesy, Scottsdale Historical Society

Below
Blacksmith George Cavalliere was the target of the first town zoning decision when the city fathers did not want his "smelly" business in town. He established his workshop on what was then the outskirts of town and now is in the heart of Old Town at the northeast corner of Brown and Second streets. Courtesy, Cavalliere Family

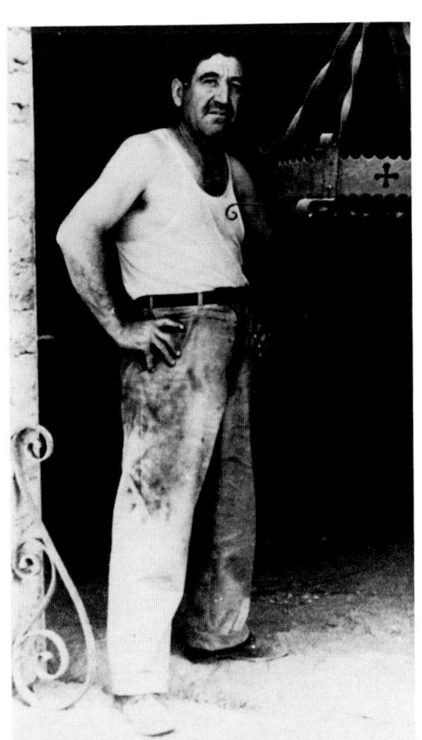

added for girls and manual training classes for boys. Both of these were conducted in the basement. Most of the students walked or rode horses until the first school bus was revved up in 1923. The driver of the canvas-covered truck was paid a dollar a day for the round trip.

A Parent-Teacher Association was organized in 1917 and was instrumental in starting and assisting with a school lunch program in 1920. It was run by Clara "Pansy" Boyer Beauchamp, who later operated the Scottsdale Cafe. She received a dollar a day to run the "cook shack" with two kerosene stoves in a tent under nearby ash trees. Teachers would collect 10 cents from pupils in the morning and give it to Mrs. Beauchamp, who would shop at Brown's general store and then start preparing the food. She made sandwiches and hot dishes (usually beans) and sold milk and fruit. Two pupils were given free lunches for serving and washing dishes.

Development now began to take place in and around the original town site, which was located south and east of the present Scottsdale and Indian School roads. In 1914 a 1,000-acre residential area named Security Acres was located west of Scott's original town site. Offered by the Arizona Securities and Investment Company, the area was promoted as "the Pasadena of Arizona." Next to develop was a 220-acre subdivision called Citrus Homes Addition, the first in the Arcadia district nearer Camelback Mountain and slightly westward toward Phoenix. Additional progress came to town thanks to Lester Mowry, who first arrived in 1917 with his farmer father and brother to escape the Texas drought. They moved on, but returned in 1919. After high school Mowry became an electrician and married Labeula Steiner. He worked on most of the major projects in the valley, including the Arizona Biltmore, Wrigley Mansion, Arizona State University, and San Carlos Hotel. He also helped install the first neon lights in Arizona, the first sound film projector, the first night baseball lights, and the first high-intensity lights at Sky Harbor Airport.

Joseph Hydukovich (later changed to Hyduke) and his 13-member family joined the community in 1919. They built a five-room frame farmhouse with a cellar, two brick fireplaces, and a sleeping porch on George Street (now Civic Center Plaza) north of Thomas Road.

An important early local business was George Cavalliere's blacksmith shop. "Cavie" and his wife, Mary Alice, had come to Arizona in 1908 from Santa Barbara after he was hired to do repair work on the massive Arizona Canal dredge and to shoe the horses and mules that pulled it. For a year the Cavallieres lived on the canal bank in one of the earliest-known mobile homes—a tin shed

Above
The home of "Madame Evans" (eastern artist Jessie Benton Evans) was the nucleus of what became Jokake Inn, the first resort in the Scottsdale area. Courtesy, Barbara Ferris

Opposite page, top
Cavalliere's blacksmith shop was built on Brown Street of adobe in 1920. It replaced the original tin building, which was constructed in 1910. Courtesy, Scottsdale Historical Society

Bottom
Sturdy Jokake Inn began as a little tearoom and then expanded into a resort that operated from the 1930s until the late 1970s. Mexicans from Scottsdale and Indians from the reservation helped build the resort. Tin ornaments were made by Barnebe Herrera and wrought-iron fixtures by George Cavalliere for the owners, Sylvia Evans and Lucy Cuthbert. Courtesy, City of Scottsdale

that was pulled from place to place on a wooden sled as the dredge moved along the canal toward the Arizona Falls.

When the canal work was done, Cavie bought one of the tin sheds and, with the help of coal-wagon driver and town constable Al Fredericks, moved it to Scottsdale to establish a blacksmith shop and ornamental iron works. That shop was the target of the small colony's first zoning decision. Cavie wanted to build it on Main Street, but the city fathers thought the smoke and smell from a smithy's shop would detract from the aesthetics of residential life. Therefore, they insisted he build on the outskirts of town. So, he launched his business at the northeast corner of present Brown Avenue and Second Street. Ironically, this location later became the heart of downtown Scottsdale. In 1920 Cavalliere added an adjacent adobe brick building that is still in use.

As a sideline Cavie ran boxing and wrestling matches in the shop, hanging burlap over the doors and windows to discourage freeloaders. Paying customers watched "Indian Tommy" Burns wrestle The Masked Marvel from Prescott.

Cavalliere also did ornamental work for the home built by Eastern artist Jessie Benton Evans, called "Madame Evans" by everyone. Her son and daughter-in-law, architect Robert Evans and his wife, Sylvia, built an adobe home nearby. In 1927 their home became the Jokake Inn, the first valley resort with Spanish and Indian architecture and art.

Sylvia Evans and a friend, Lucy Cuthbert, opened a small tearoom in which they offered a 50-cent luncheon consisting of a chicken salad sandwich, devil's food cake, and tea. It emerged as Scottsdale's second in-town resort. Earlier, Mildred Bartholow and Imogene Ireland, two single sisters who also had started with a tearoom, had opened an inn called The Adobe House in the former Blount home and first school.

The desert had changed drastically from Scott's early vista of barren sands to green fields with some 10,000 acres under cultivation. There was a great demand for cotton during World War I when the supply from Egypt was cut off, and Scottsdale's fields were producing high-quality cotton. The long-staple strain was needed in the production of new balloon-type vehicle tires and in fabric airplane wings. Increased cotton production meant that farmers needed more field hands, so they began to sponsor Mexican immigrant families. Among these immigrants were the Tomas Corrals.

Dairy farming also was prevalent, and fresh milk was home-delivered for five cents a quart. A cheese factory that had been established in 1914 in part of the former Blount home was producing 178 pounds a day.

Storekeeper E.O. Brown, who with partner Wilford Hayden had made his first shipment of beef to California markets in 1910, established the D.C. (Desert Camp) Ranch north of Scottsdale. The cattle were driven down from the mountains for a final fattening on alfalfa in Scottsdale holding pens before going to market. It was common to see cattle filling three blocks along dusty Paradise Avenue and posing a hazard to cotton pickers and schoolchildren.

Though the class of 1917 had only three graduating students, the ceremony in The Little Red Schoolhouse was complete with a valedictorian, white dresses, and a program. When the population grew because of the influx of cotton workers, two redwood buildings were erected in 1918 and 1920 to supplement the original red brick schoolhouse. By 1918 the schools had four teachers and a combined enrollment of 165. In 1920 there were six teachers and 410 pupils. Enrollment continued to grow until there were 10 teachers in 1922 and 14 by 1927.

Grade school principal L.O. DuRoss became Scottsdale's first school superintendent in 1923, the same year Scottsdale High School opened. The first Scottsdale High School graduating class in the spring of 1923 (before the building was completed) had only three graduates: Hunter Chesnutt, Murle Miller, and her brother, William Miller.

When the eight-classroom Scottsdale Grammar School (later named Loloma Elementary) was built in 1928, Garland White became the principal, supervising an 11-member teaching staff. He later succeeded DuRoss as superintendent. The Little Red Schoolhouse then was designated the Coronado School. It was the community center for the Mexican barrio and was used for three grades of Mexican-American pupils to help them adjust to the new culture before joining their Anglo friends in fourth grade.

Grace Thomas, who married local rancher Arthur Crews, taught Scottsdale pupils for 28 years, from January 1929 to May 1957, starting at the Little Red Schoolhouse. She personally went door-to-door in the barrio to encourage Mexican-American and Yaqui families to send their children to school. Then she helped the youngsters with language problems so they could enter integrated classes.

The schoolhouse later was converted to town hall offices and the justice of the peace court. Then it held the city library. The long-useful building was saved from being razed for downtown redevelopment in the 1970s through the efforts of the chamber of commerce and longtime residents. The campaign was supported by the community's newspaper, the *Scottsdale Daily Progress*, which launched a fund-raising campaign that included donations of pennies from schoolchildren. In 1973 the old but still-useful

Opposite page, top left
The first graduating class of Scottsdale High School poses for an informal photo near the school. The class was composed of William Miller (left), Hunter Chesnutt (right), and Murle Miller (rear). Courtesy, Scottsdale Historical Society

Top right
The 1936 Scottsdale High School team strikes a photogenic pose for posterity on the school lawn. Courtesy, Mr. and Mrs. Lester Mowry

Bottom
Entertainment was the name of the game for high school coeds in the 1930s, and to be chosen for the cast of a play or musical was a big honor. When each class put on a play during the school year, the Scottsdale High School auditorium would be crowded with townspeople since there was not even a local movie theater at the time. Courtesy, Thelma Steiner Holveck/Labeula Steiner Mowry

building, preserved at the northwest end of the Scottsdale Mall, became the home of the Scottsdale Chamber of Commerce.

For years the schoolhouse bell had called everyone to ecumenical services and Sunday school classes at the schoolhouse. Because of the religious persuasion of its founder, Scottsdale's early residents were mostly Baptists, but there also were Methodists and Presbyterians. The first denominational church came into being in 1912 when the Baptists decided to organize with others from Phoenix and Tempe. They met in June at the Reverend Verner Vanderhoof's home, and the first baptismal service took place that Easter in an irrigation ditch at the southeast corner of Scottsdale and Indian School roads.

The First Baptist Church building was dedicated in 1918 at the southwest corner of Brown Avenue and Indian School Road on land donated by Chaplain Scott's widow. Scottsdale Methodist Church was organized in 1924 by 22 people meeting in a rented store at the southwest corner of Main Street and Scottsdale Road. A red-brick building was erected in 1929 at the northwest corner of Main Street and Marshall Way as the congregation's first real home. The town's first Catholic church—Our Lady of Perpetual Help—was built in 1933 on Brown Avenue. Emilio Corral, with the aid of his brother, Jesus, who spoke English, supervised the construction of the adobe-brick building.

New growth also was coming to downtown Scottsdale, which for many years had been no more than the intersection of Brown Avenue and Main Street. As the demands of a growing population were placed on business, downtown Scottsdale began to expand. In 1909 E.O. Brown had replaced J.L. Davis' 1897-vintage frame store building with one of cement block, and in 1920 he added a much-appreciated ice plant. In 1950, after Brown's 32 years at the location, the store became the first arts and crafts center in Scottsdale. Later it was expanded as the Kiva Craft Center on Fifth Avenue.

Johnny Rose had come to town in 1914 and had built a frame structure to house a candy shop and poolroom at the northeast corner of Brown and Main. Rose had a checkered business career. He was arrested for running a "disorderly house" (brothel) and permitting underage drinking and open gambling in his poolroom. After he married in 1917, however, he settled down to legitimate business. His store sign at that time read: "John Rose, Fancy Groceries, Shoe Repairing, Barber Shop, Pool Hall, Ice Cream, Confectionary and Soft Drinks."

In 1923, to compete with new businesses that had opened in his area—another general store, soft drink emporium, barber shop, and pool hall—Rose dug out a full basement, razed the frame

Opposite page, top
A Sunday School gathering took place during a picnic at the Hayden Ranch about 1910. In the front row, from left, are: Hugh Hayden (on milk can), Alvin Brown, Stanley Ellis Thomas, James Vanderhoof (small child in front), Wilford "Boy" Hayden, Jr., George Thomas, and Ellsworth Brown. The second row includes: Frank Last (Scottsdale Grammar School teacher), Mrs. Wilford Hayden, (Sunday School teacher), Gussie Hayden, and Ethel Hayden. Finally, in the third row, are: May Vanderhoof, Frances Ward, Mary Keene Graves, Helen Hayden. Courtesy, Emmajeane Harris

Bottom
Scottsdale's first Catholic church, Our Lady of Perpetual Help, was built of 14,000 adobe bricks made by hand by the town's Mexican residents. Earth was mixed with straw and water by foot-stamping, cut with hoes, and poured into molds. This 1950 photograph shows the north-side addition with its arched doorways. The building now houses the Scottsdale Symphony Orchestra. Courtesy, Scottsdale Historical Society

store, and put up a two-story building faced with dazzling glazed-white imported brick. The building stood out among the other plain red brick structures. He offered billiards and pool and Saturday-night silent movies for a nickel admission.

In 1929, the same year neighboring Tempe incorporated as a city, Jew Chew Song moved his family to Scottsdale from Chandler. He bought Rose's pool hall and in it opened J. Chew's grocery store. The shop, with a rear upstairs apartment for the parents and their six children, carried Four Roses Flour from the Hayden Mills in Tempe, locally grown produce, soda pop, and donuts. Later, when it became more profitable to sell Mexican curios, the store's name was changed to Mexican Imports. Still in business today, it is run by John Song, one of the sons who was born in Scottsdale. Another of the sons, Jackson Song, opened China Lil's restaurant in 1963 in a small adobe building nearby, then expanded into a large new building on the redeveloped mall. Since selling that location, he revived the name J. Chew's for his small cafe at the rear of the Mexican Imports building.

The favorable business climate was further encouraged between 1920 and 1921 by several technological improvements. Brown's Scottsdale Ginning Company began its cotton operation on Second Street south of Brown with the gin shipped from England and assembled by Charles Coldwell. The Scottsdale Light and Power Company was incorporated with Mort Kimsey's prodding, noting that "the women were tired of coal oil lamps," so power was connected from the Arizona Falls generating plant. Four streetlights were installed at the town's four main corners—Brown and Main, Scottsdale and Main, Scottsdale and Indian School, and Indian School and Brown.

In 1920 the number of small businesses increased from three to nine. The initial trio included E.O. Brown's general store, Johnny Rose's Pool Hall, and the McComb Brothers store. Then added along Brown and Main were Farmers' State Bank, A.F. Mahoney Mercantile, Sterling Drug, Herron and Walker Barbershop and Pool Hall, Eckley's Soft Drink Emporium and Stage Office, and Kubelsky's Clothing Store (originally the Boston Store, run by Marshall and Lillian Kubelsky, uncle and aunt of comedian Jack Benny).

A.F. Mahoney Mercantile opened in 1920 as a general store on the east side of Brown, north of Main. The adobe building later became a feed store, a garage, and then the Basket House. The original adobe wall still can be seen in the upper space between that building and Mexican Imports.

The Sterling Drug Store opened in 1921 at the northwest corner of Brown and Main, and later became the Scottsdale Pharmacy in the building now occupied by Saba's Western Wear Store. Just around the corner, a U.S. post office was built in 1928. Porter's Western Wear now occupies this building.

Earl Shipp started out as a stock and carryout boy and meat cutter at the two-story Byer's Market at the northwest corner of Scottsdale Road and Main Street. He bought out the owner in 1935, changed the store's name to Earl's Market, and operated it until 1973. That year he leased the property to First National (now Interstate) Bank.

The first automobiles, Wilford Hayden's Buick and E.O. Brown's Dodge, were brought to town in 1912. Walter Smith, who opened the town's first auto agency in 1918, sold Chevrolets, and grocer Brown installed a fuel pump in front of his store. One day, after a car accident on Main Street, the city fathers established a parking regulation that allowed drivers to angle park only, one deep, in front of businesses. The Indians, on the other hand, preferred to tie up their horse-drawn wagons under shade trees north of the center of town on First Avenue. When businesses were established there, the area became known as Pima Plaza.

By 1926 Kimsey's Scottsdale Service Company, a Ford agency and service station at the northeast corner of Scottsdale Road and Main Street, was doing work on Model A's. Farm mechanic Elliott "Scotty" Scott moved in from his farm and opened a blacksmith and machine shop at the southeast corner of Scottsdale Road and First Avenue. Tool-and-die maker Gabe Brooks, Scott's friend and an early settler at the Powder Horn Ranch, later also moved to town.

The town's first newspaper, the *Scottsdale Bulletin,* was published in 1922 by Roy George, a playwright for whom George Street was named (now Civic Center Plaza).

But not even in the expansive era of the 1920s was it all work for Scottsdale residents. Small pleasures included canoeing on the Arizona Canal and attending rodeos put on by Indians from the Fort McDowell Reservation in a vacant lot behind Vice President Marshall's home. Medicine shows and carnivals were staged on a vacant lot on Brown Street. One year Mary Keene Graves beat all the cowboys to win the Thanksgiving town rodeo racing events on her horse Ruggles. On New Year's Eve, the Pima Indians put on all-night costumed dances that were attended by many residents. Croquet was a favorite yard activity, while the affluent enjoyed polo at the Ingleside Inn.

Scottsdale's sports fans rooted for the town baseball team, the Blue Socks, affectionately called the Scottsdale "Blues." Teams played on Sunday afternoons at fields without bleachers, with fans sitting on the ground or the running boards of their cars. There

PORTER'S

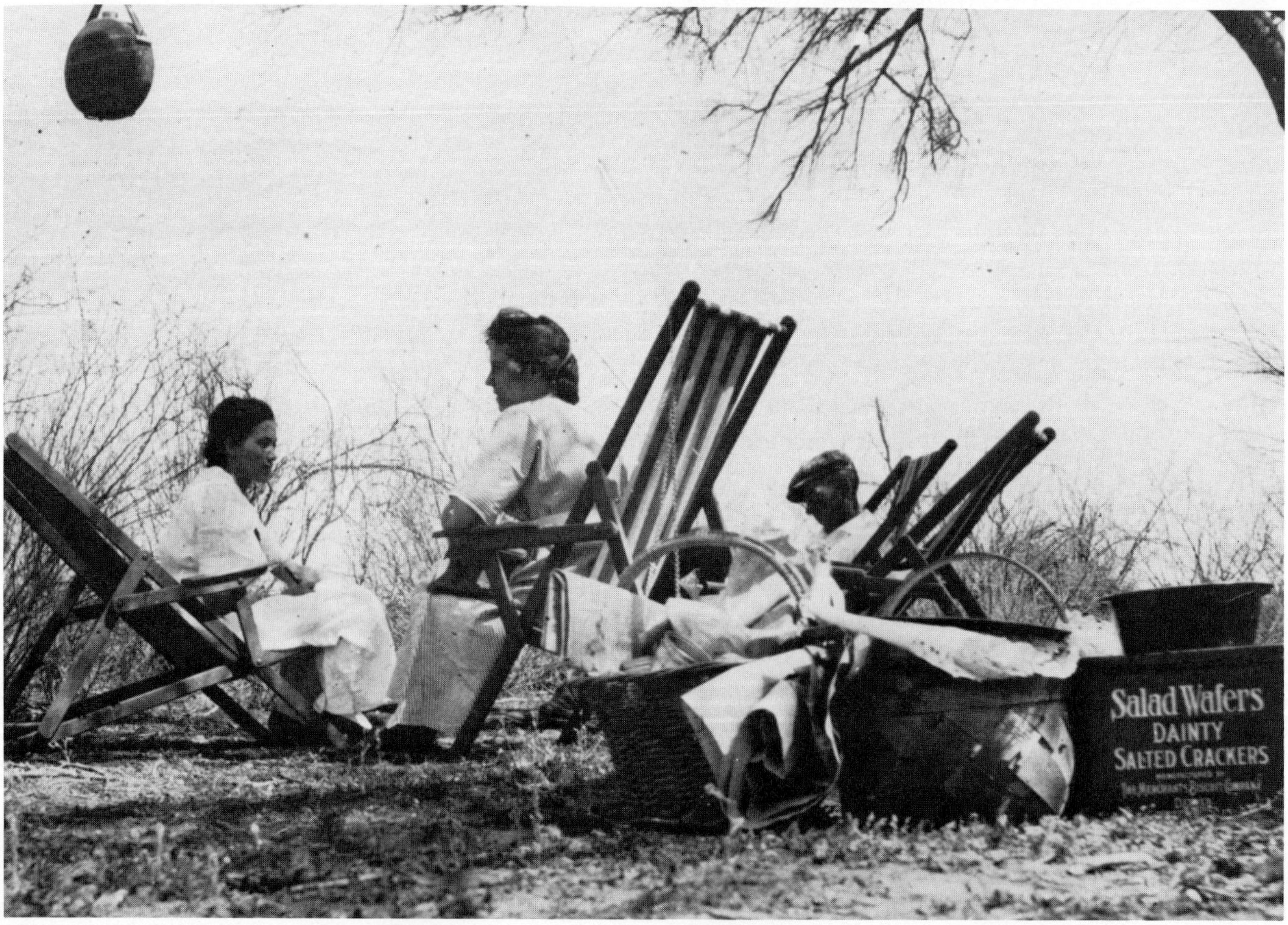

Opposite page, top left
Scottsdale's first post office building, constructed in 1928, had apartments on the second floor. By the late 1940s, the building was in use as Porter's Western Wear Store on the west side of Brown Avenue, just north of Main Street. Courtesy, Scottsdale Historical Society

Top right
The general store was not only a place to buy needed food and supplies, but also a meeting place to exchange news and gossip in the early days of the town's development. This scene from E.O. Brown Mercantile was one repeated in many similar stores. Courtesy, Scottsdale Historical Society

Bottom
A picnic on the desert was a pleasure during balmy winter days. Mort Kimsey (right) brought along reading material to pass the time before the food was unpacked from baskets and hampers. Water was kept cool in a canteen hanging in the shade of a mesquite tree. Courtesy, William L. Kimsey

also was a girls' softball team sparked by the Steiner sisters and managed by Mort Kimsey, who also coached the men's team.

Residents who could afford it would leave for several weeks or months during the summer, traveling north to mountain communities for cooler temperatures or to the West Coast for ocean breezes. Those who remained slept at night in tree-shaded yards or on screened porches. Some wrapped themselves in wet sheets and hoped they'd fall asleep before the fabric was dry. In the late 1920s evaporative or "swamp" coolers were introduced and installed in many businesses. Most homeowners built their own coolers from a wooden frame fitted with excelsior, a fan or a small motor with fan blades attached.

During Prohibition, Phoenix newspapers reported frequent raids by local authorities as they destroyed home stills to enforce the law. An article on December 14, 1922, in *The Arizona Republican*, reported: "Federal prohibition enforcement officers 'dusted the corners' of Scottsdale yesterday—corners which they overlooked in the fall house cleaning in the northeast section of the valley last Saturday." The story related how a visit to one ranch resulted in "a large quantity of liquor seized, including four gallons of raisin mash in a high state of fermentation" and the arrest of the producing rancher.

The economic woes of the Depression years in the early 1930s affected the remote little town. Cotton farmers capitulated to wage demands after a strike by Mexican workers who wanted a half-cent per pound increase to two cents for picking. The bleakest moment came when Scottsdale's only bank, Farmers' State, closed on March 2, 1933, for a "bank holiday" hastily called by Governor B.B. Moeur. It never reopened, although all its depositors later were paid off.

Because the Depression hit the small community so hard, the National Recovery Administration stepped in to help businesses stay afloat. One NRA beneficiary in town was J.T. Willmoth, who opened a grocery store in 1930 at the southeast corner of First Street and Scottsdale Road.

By 1932 there were about 30 businesses serving a population of about 2,000. Still, many residents were unable to pay their bills, and some farmers lost their acreage to the Federal Land Bank and were forced to move on. Those who remained willingly pooled their resources. Families gathered occasionally for mulligan stew parties on the desert, with each person bringing a can of some vegetable to toss into the community cookpot. Working together, they would survive.

CHAPTER THREE

Evolution of an Arts Colony

George Ellis (pictured here in 1935) built a number of homes on the north edge of the community of Scottsdale, many of which were bought by artists who moved into the area. Located near the Crosscut Canal, the area was given the spoof designation of "the West Bank." Courtesy, Rachel Ellis

Because of the hard times, more and more people left Scottsdale to try to start life anew elsewhere. The newly organized Scottsdale Chamber of Commerce, which had been housed in the Farmers' State Bank, closed in 1933 when the bank did. Not long after, Rudolph Lamfrom, a member of the school board, opened a check and currency exchange in the defunct bank building, also setting up his insurance and real-estate offices there. The business later was purchased by Al and Rosa Lindsey.

Many residents lost mortgaged land, including the Steiner family, who lost their 110 acres. The now-widowed mother and her two daughters moved in 1928 to a smaller piece of farm property consisting of 40 acres near 68th Street and McDowell Road. It had no electricity or drinking water, so 12-year-old Thelma learned to drive the family car so she could go to Oscar Sullivan's well north of the canal on Scottsdale Road or to the redwood pipeline on the reservation to bring back huge milk cans filled with water. "We never had drinking water where we lived, and when we had to move, we were lucky to eat and have shoes," she recalled. Farm families bartered fruit or eggs and chickens for grocery staples and meat. Fortunately, those were the days when hamburger cost 10 cents a pound or three pounds for a quarter.

After her mother died, Thelma was hired in 1935 by the Works Projects Administration to dispense food from the back room of the Justice Court, formerly the Methodist church, at the southwest corner of Main Street and Scottsdale Road.

Despite the ebbing national economy, valley resorts were being built to attract still-wealthy easterners seeking an escape from winter's ravages. Big Phoenix hotels such as the Westward Ho, Arizona Biltmore, and Wigwam, all built in 1929, soon had competition from Jokake Inn, which expanded from its original few guest rooms and added the twin adobe towers that are still landmarks. Many of Scottsdale's Mexican residents worked on the adobe building project, including the Corrals, Rangels, and tinsmith Barnebe Herrera, who created light fixtures and table ornaments. The little inn soon became widely known and was frequented by prominent easterners such as the Astors and Rockefellers. The young Mexican men and women who lived in Scottsdale found jobs as maids, kitchen workers, and bus boys.

Henry C. Wick III, who joined the Judson School faculty in 1938, has been director and owner since 1946. The school's original red tile-roofed tower still stands among the additions to the campus of Arizona's oldest independent college preparatory school. The first polo matches in the valley were played on these fields in 1928. Courtesy, Barbara and Henry Wick III

The founding of Judson School for Boys in 1928 by George A. Judson, superintendent of the Osborn School District in Phoenix, and the opening of Jokake School for Girls by Robert Evans in 1933 brought more easterners by train to the desert Southwest. Judson School, Arizona's oldest independent college preparatory school, was nationally renowned for its championship tennis and polo teams. Yale graduate Henry C. Wick III came from Cleveland, Ohio, to join the Judson faculty in 1938. He became director and owner in 1946.

Judson School attracted students from the social register, including the meat-packing families of the Swifts, Morrells, and Armours. In later years the school enrolled children of other prominent people, including Michael Reagan (whose father Ronald was a graduation speaker twice), the Prince of Kuwait, and the daughters of U.S. Senator Barry Goldwater. More than 30 countries are represented in the student body, and all international holidays are celebrated.

Late in 1934, Judson School for Girls was built to the southwest of the original school. It was operated for two years by Judson's daughter, Jeannette, before the school was converted into an annex for the boys' school. Then, in 1937, Mark and Janet Gruber of Montana purchased the school and turned it into El Chorro Lodge.

Camelback Inn, which joined the resort scene in 1936, was built for $100,000 on the southern slope of Mummy Mountain by John C. Lincoln, president of the Cleveland Electric Company in Ohio. It opened in time for Christmas with ex-Wigwam Resort manager Jack Stewart taking over. Rooms cost $10 to $25 a day, and the main topic in the dining room was the abdication from the British throne of the Duke of Windsor for his beloved Wallis Warfield Simpson, a divorcee. Stewart and his wife, Louise, later bought the resort with its Indian-theme decor and small cottages named for different species of cactus. They also bought the first in a succession of pet burros, each named Snowball.

Kiami Lodge, built on the west side of Scottsdale Road just north of Chaparral Road, was another resort popular with eastern visitors who came to ride horseback, play tennis and golf, attend polo games at the Ingleside, and watch thoroughbred horse races at the Arizona Downs track, which was located on the grounds until the late 1950s. Among the guests were the Raymond Rubicams of New York's Young and Rubicam ad agency and other successful businessmen. Many of them stayed on to establish new companies, thus bringing further development and popularity to Scottsdale.

Others came to pursue more basic livelihoods. Builder Duncan MacDonald, for whom MacDonald Drive was named, constructed

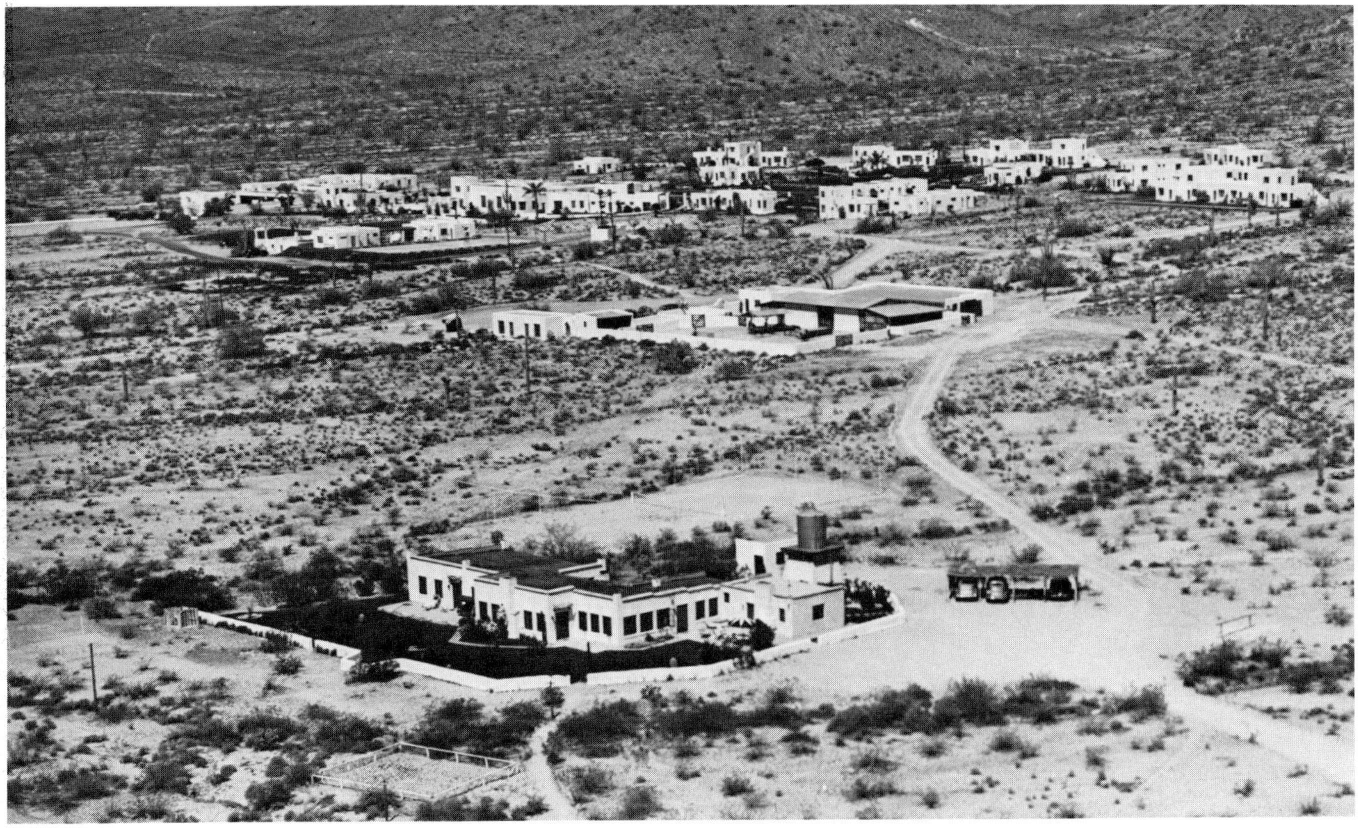

Camelback Flashes
Down in our Cholla, dampest spot on the desert, Ed Russell and Jerry Baker, entertain at Camelback Inn for their Phoenix friends. A good supply of Scotch and Bonded Bourbons is available at reasonable prices. With our new cactus dining room, we are in a position all winter to handle Phoenix dining parties with or without advance reservations. Those who entertain at Camelback will be delighted with the food and the pleasant, deft service. Special Sunday dinner at noon, $3.50; Buffet Sunday night, $3.00; Luncheon, week-days, $2.50; dinner, week-days, $3.50. For those who need lodging a few rooms are available for guests at the Inn from now until January 6.
CAMELBACK INN
PHOENIX ARIZONA
Under the friendly management of Jack Stewart

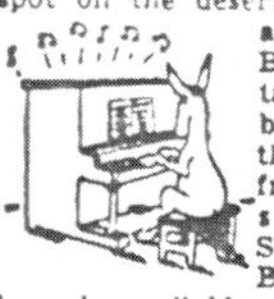

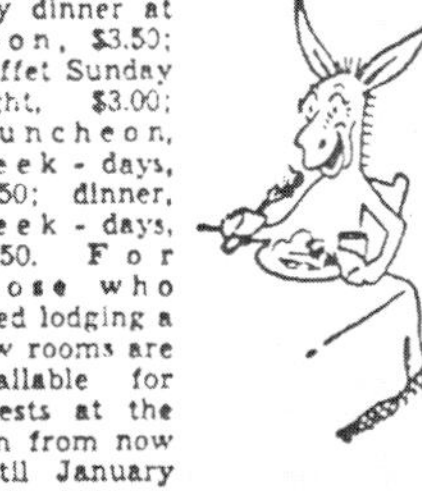

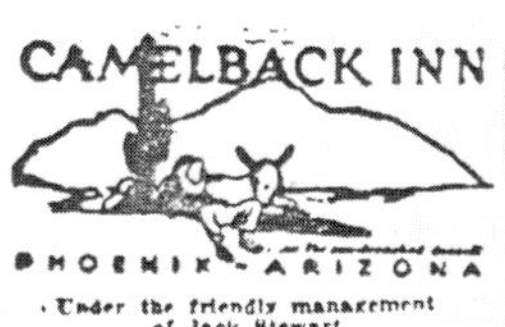

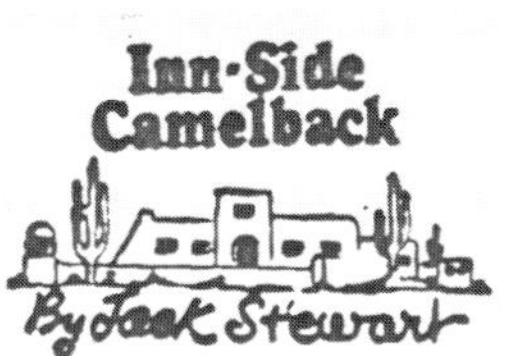

Inn-Side Camelback
By Jack Stewart
You can start the New Year out right by having dinner at Camelback Inn either at 12:30 to 2:00 or at 6:30 to 8:00 p. m. on January 1.
Snowball, our burro, says a trip to the desert is good for the soul and, we might add, for the stomach, too, providing you dine at Camelback. The food is marvelous and the complete dinner price, $3.50—reasonable if you seek the best. Please phone 5-4741 for reservations.
CAMELBACK INN
PHOENIX ARIZONA

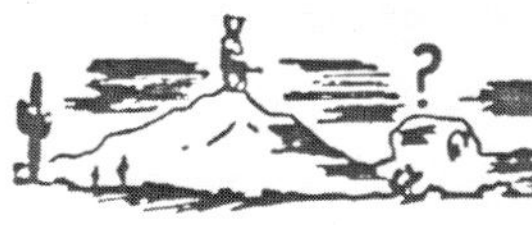

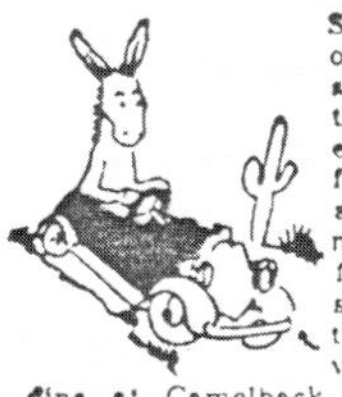

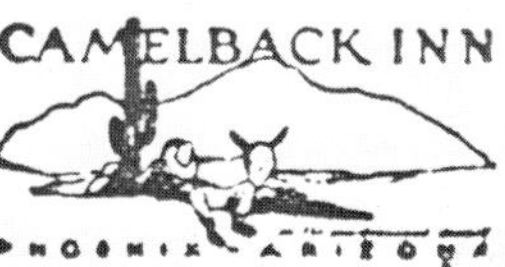

Above
El Chorro Lodge opened in 1937 after the facility had been the Judson School for Girls for several years. The lodge, with its distinctive beehive fireplaces, was an attraction to town residents and tourists alike. The El Chorro is seen here at lower center and the two-year-old Camelback Inn is located toward the top on the southern slope of Mummy Mountain. The Camelback offered rooms ranging from $10 to $25 a day in the early 1930s. Courtesy, Joe and Evie Miller

Left
A white mule named Snowball was the leading character in a series of advertisements in the Arizona Republic *in December of 1946. The little newsy-notes columns touted a special Sunday dinner for three dollars and fifty cents and weekday lunches for two dollars and fifty cents, encouraging "a trip to the desert" as being "good for the soul, and, we might add, for the stomach, too." Courtesy, City of Scottsdale*

a model home for a proposed subdivision in the mid-1930s at the southwest corner of what is now MacDonald Drive and Invergordon Road. George Ellis, an architect and government surveyor who had come through the Scottsdale area in the early 1930s on assignment, returned to marry teacher Rachel Murdock and build an unusual home. He had learned that "The Big Redwood Line," a Verde River Water Project pipeline, was constructed of two-inch-thick redwood slabs banded in steel. Because it leaked, the partially buried line had been abandoned. The enterprising Ellis, however, dug up the wood and built his house from it. Some of the redwood was used for doors at Camelback Inn and paneled walls in the Scottsdale YMCA office building. Ellis also was known for his adobe-building skills. He erected 14 houses in the desert west of the canal between MacDonald and Lincoln drives, many of which still stand.

The artists began to come too, attracted by the clean air and sunny skies. Philip Curtis first lived at the corner of 70th Street and Indian School Road on a property so overgrown with vegetation that it was called "Tiger Jungle" by the mail carrier. Curtis later moved into one of the Ellis-built homes in the area near the Arizona Canal and named the dirt road Cattle Track because it had been an early route for livestock drives to the mountains. Artist Avis Read turned her Ellis home into the Stable Gallery on MacDonald Drive. After more artists came, they paid tribute to the canal by calling their secluded colony "The West Bank."

Architect Frank Lloyd Wright had come west in 1927 to work on a desert resort project in Chandler, but it was a victim of the Depression and he never received his fee. After returning to his Spring Glen, Wisconsin, headquarters and a well-paying contract, Wright and his wife, Olgivanna, came back in 1937 to set up a rustic outdoor camp at the foot of the McDowell Mountains. This was the first portion of the architectural school that became Taliesin West. Life was spartan during the school's early days—no water, no electricity, no heating, and no plumbing—with only tents pitched in the desert until the first rubblestone buildings could be constructed by staff and students. The teaching-and-arts center became Scottsdale's first to be listed on the National Register of Historic Places in 1976. In July 1982 it was designated a U.S. Landmark.

Wright's creative presence made a name for Scottsdale, attracting more artists to make the community their home base. One was former working cowboy Lon Megargee, whose creations included commercial work for the Stetson hat company and a series of paintings illustrating cowboy life created for the A-l Brewing

Opposite page, top left
Philip Curtis came to Scottsdale in the 1930s and became internationally known for his work. He later became a driving force in the city's fine arts commission, and in 1983 was named Arizona Artist of the Year. Courtesy, Jose Y. Bermudez

Top right
An early view of internationally known Taliesin West, architect Frank Lloyd Wright's southwestern headquarters, shows the rough rubblestone buildings the staff and students constructed from the surrounding environment. In the late 1930s and early 1940s, the roofs were covered with canvas that could let in the air while providing shade from the sunlight. Courtesy, Frank Lloyd Wright Foundation

Bottom left
This house at 77th Street and Thomas Road was built to the specifications of nationally known sculptress Mathilde Schaefer of New York after she came to Scottsdale in 1936. She joined an already viable art colony in a rural setting and met artist Lew Davis. The couple was married soon after. Davis painted this mural on the north patio wall of their home. Courtesy, Suzanne Starr/Scottsdale Daily Progress

Bottom right
Lew Davis was one of the original artists involved in the Arizona Craft Center, the nucleus of what was to become Scottsdale's reputation for arts. Courtesy, Scottsdale Daily Progress

Opposite page, top
Wood-carver Phillips Sanderson was one of the artists who discovered Scottsdale in the early 1940s. At the time it was so quiet and unremarkable that he likened it to a ghost town. Sanderson later joined other artisans to form the Arizona Craftsmen Council at Brown and Main in E.O. Brown's former grocery store. Sanderson specialized in carving Indian figures that represented Arizona tribes. Later he received a commission for work for Valley National Bank. Courtesy, Wes Segner

Bottom
The phenomenon of snow in central Arizona in 1937 was a surprise and delight for everyone. These children of Tom and Ruby Willmoth —Gwendolyn and Norma—frolicked in the odd stuff, which stayed on the ground for a few hours. Camelback Mountain is in the background. Courtesy, George Willmoth

Company of Arizona. Many of them, including *Cowboy's Dream*, were placed in bars around the West. Megargee built a home, Casa Hermosa, with three-foot-thick adobe walls. It later became a resort called the Hermosa Inn, which still operates. In June 1937 the Arizona Painters and Sculptors organized at the Hotel Adams in Phoenix. Among those present were sculptor Mathilde Schaefer and artist Lew Davis. They soon were joined by others, including painter Oscar Strobel, Jr., woodcarver Phillips Sanderson, and painter Philip Curtis, who in later years helped develop the city's fine arts collection and in 1983 was named Arizona's Artist of the Year. All helped to cultivate Scottsdale's roots as a haven for artists and craftsmen.

The winter of 1937 brought heavy snow to this usually sunny little Southwestern community. A couple of inches fell and stayed on the ground for a few hours, amazing the adults and delighting the children. Even the cotton bolls in the farm fields were whiter as they became filled with snow.

At the dawn of the next decade, the U.S. Census put the population of Scottsdale at 740. That was the year William Schrader, Sr., established a 110-acre farm at the southwest corner of Indian School and Hayden roads. His son and namesake later became a mayor of Scottsdale.

Malcolm White, who had come as a child from his native Glendale, Arizona, in 1921, bought Glen Conrad's All-Rite Cafe on Brown Avenue in 1941. The following year he bought a service station at the southeast corner of Main and Scottsdale Road and turned it into Whitey's Cafe and Bar. Longtime residents tell about the time White's friend, stunt rider Dick Griffith, rode his horse right through the front door.

White is among those credited with conceiving and encouraging Scottsdale's Old West architectural style with its wooden sidewalks and posts and shingled roofs over the walkways. He later leased his corner cafe to Claudia Ogden and another woman, who promptly changed its name to the more feminine Pink Pony. It soon became a popular local "watering hole." When former bartender Charlie Briley bought the cafe in 1950, he retained the name. After he lost his lease, he moved the restaurant to its present location a few doors south on Scottsdale Road, where it is known for the framed caricatures of customers done by former Disney Studio artist Don Barclay.

Phillips Sanderson recalled that when he first came to Scottsdale in 1941, "it looked just like an old ghost town that was about ready to fall down." The Sandersons lived with the Schaefer-Davises in a large house with two studios and living quarters for two families. After the war, they established the Arizona Crafts building with

Lloyd Kiva New, a leather craftsman, was the key force behind the Arizona Craftsmen Council and, later, the development of Fifth Avenue as a center for arts and crafts and unusual shops. He first became known for ladies' soft shoulder bags made from reindeer leather, which were adaptations of the colorful Indian medicine man's pouch. He later expanded into handwoven woolens and other leather goods. Courtesy, City of Scottsdale

the help of Tom Darlington, who met with several artists including the Davises, Sandersons, leather-artisan Lloyd Kiva New, silversmith Wes Segner, and calligrapher-photographer Leonard Yuschik. Darlington and K.T. Palmer, both of whom later developed the town of Carefree to the north, leased space to the artists in the old E.O. Brown market and former ice house at the southwest corner of Brown and Main.

The town's craft center, styled after similar artists' areas in Mexico, housed working studio-shops for artisans. The small shops were centered around a skylighted patio planted with greenery, each shop with a door opening out onto the center area. Here tourists could watch the artists before they bought their works. Hand-wrought wares for sale included ceramics, pottery, sculptures, paintings, leather, Indian jewelry and artifacts, and silver items.

The advent of World War II had a major effect on the little town. Scottsdale had been growing very slowly until servicemen were assigned to four airfields in the valley, including Thunderbird II in north Scottsdale. Hundreds of civilian flight instructors were imported to train cadets for the Army Air Corps at that field, plus two in Mesa (Falcon and Williams) and one in Glendale (Thunderbird I).

Scottsdale men of every life-style went into the armed forces, among them artist Lew Davis, cowboy George Thomas, Jr., and Judson schoolteacher Henry C. Wick III. The enrollment at Scottsdale High dropped from 174 in 1941 to 131 the next year. Some students quit school to go to work because wages were higher, while others joined the service. There had been 40 graduates in the class of 1940, but in 1942 there were only 17.

As more and more local young men fought overseas, hometown Red Cross volunteer Labeula Steiner Mowry took on the sad task of delivering telegrams informing families that their loved ones were missing or killed in action. Grace Crews' son, Private Stanley Crews, was captured in 1943 by the Japanese and died in a Manila, Philippines, prison camp. Subsequently the local Veterans of Foreign Wars Post was named in his honor. That same year the whole community was praised for having the highest per capita sale of war bonds in the nation: 331 of 350 residents had purchased $82,000 in bonds.

One peculiar segment of Scottsdale's wartime population was a group of German naval personnel interned in a prisoner-of-war camp at Papago Park near McDowell Road and 64th Street. In December 1943 a passenger train brought the first contingent of 400 prisoners, some of whom were hard-line Nazis. As many as 4,000 at one time were interned there during the next few years, some working on local agricultural projects, picking citrus, and cleaning ditch banks.

What has been called *The Great Escape* took place the second year, when the prisoners dug a 170-foot-tunnel under a 20-foot shaft through rock and desert caliche. Using only small coal-stove shovels it took them months to dig the tunnel. But on Christmas Eve of 1944, 60 prisoners vanished from camp and scattered into the desert night. About 35 of them were apprehended almost immediately. Others, discouraged by cold and rain, gave up and sought shelter in Tempe homes. Still others, traveling by night and resting by day, made it clear to Mexico, where they were turned in.

In the post-World War II era, Scottsdale reverted to its normally sedate pattern of growth. Retired chemist Murle Cheney (for whom Cheney Road was named) had purchased land for $40 an acre in the area which became McCormick Ranch in 1942. He lived in a home on Mummy Mountain and raised Arabian horses on the ranchland below. "He had a white Buick convertible, and he'd wear an all-white suit and hat," recalled Bill Kimsey. Cheney sold 160 acres to the Fowler McCormicks (of McCormick Reaper and International Harvester) in the mid-1940s. Mrs. McCormick, who bred Arabian horses and Angus cattle on the land, soon purchased more property until the family owned 4,200 acres, 600 of it used for farming grain. She also developed Paradise Park on Pima Road for a horse showgrounds.

A dozen Arabian horse owners established the Arabian Horse Association in 1952, conducting the first All-Arabian Horse Show in 1955. There were about 100 horses entered in that first event, which cost its backers $7,500. Three decades later that amount wouldn't be enough for stall rentals for the week-long show and auction.

In 1948 Earl Shipp moved into a new store building at the southwest corner of Main Street and Scottsdale Road. He relocated again, in 1954, to the southwest corner of Scottsdale Road and First Street, the site today of First Interstate Bank. An early developer, Shipp built the town's first three privately owned post offices. The one constructed in 1945 later became part of Lute's Pharmacy on Scottsdale Road south of Main Street.

Luther "Lute" Wasbotten came from Milwaukee and in 1949 purchased the Scottsdale Pharmacy from Shirley Brown and Earl Shipp. His motto was "right next to the post office, and just as reliable." Wasbotten was a colorful downtown figure, easily identified by his trademarks: a Western shirt and boots and a silver bola tie fashioned into a mortar and pestle with the pharmaceutical "Rx" engraved upon it. Lute's soda fountain tradition of freshly

Silversmith Wes Segner was among the artisans who worked in view of browsing tourists in the Arizona Craftsmen Council at the corner of Brown and Main in the 1940s. Segner later developed his own craft colony and also became the president of the reactivated chamber of commerce. Courtesy, Wes Segner

baked pies attracted visiting celebrities, among them U.S. Vice President Hubert Humphrey and his wife, film stars John Wayne and Lucille Ball, band leader Ted Fiorito, actor Don Ameche, and columnist Walter Winchell. The latter two lived in Scottsdale for many years.

Attorney William Messinger, because of his own health, had brought his family from Grand Rapids, Michigan, in 1942. He operated a ranch and dairy farm at the southeast corner of Indian School and Miller Road until the early 1960s, where the Messingers raised dairy cattle, chickens, and turkeys, and grew watermelons.

Emmette V. Graham, a college advertising graduate, had arrived in Phoenix on the last day of 1929 with only $45 in his pocket. In 1945, after serving in the Air Force, he moved to Scottsdale. Graham started the valley's first advertising agency and put together some of the biggest real-estate deals in Scottsdale and the valley (including what is now McCormick Ranch). In 1930 he designated the alfalfa field that became Phoenix airport as Sky Harbor and coined the phrase "Valley of the Sun." He also helped develop Fifth Avenue.

The Picket Fence, Scottsdale's very first gift shop, was an omen of things to come. It opened as an annex to Earl's Market on the north side of West Main Street soon after the war ended and symbolized the first step in the town's transition from small, rural community to tourist-oriented city.

Scottsdale's first shopping center didn't take shape until 1947. The Village Patio, on Lottie Seidel's former property on the north side of Main Street (now the Portofino Theater), included these stores: Boots and Saddles (western wear), Patio Book Shop (books, stationery, and gifts), Patio Pantry (candles and gourmet foods), Patio Fashions (custom-made casual clothing), Tres Jolie (beauty salon), and La Merienda Cafe (Mexican food). Ranchera Fashions, next door to the Patio, specialized in denims and cottons. In those days nearly all the shops closed by late May for the summer.

More resorts expanded Scottsdale's attraction for tourists. Paradise Inn was opened in 1946 by retired architect Robert Evans, who had sold his share of Jokake Inn to his former wife, Mrs. Ronald (Sylvia) Byrnes, the previous year. Then came the openings of Casa Blanca Inn, the former Donald Kellogg home with its distinctive minaret, that same year; the Royal Palms Inn on East Camelback Road in 1948; and the Ride 'n' Rock Ranch (now the site of the Radisson Resort) in 1949. Although the long-established inns were charging $25 to $50 a day for room and meals, the average El Chorro Lodge rate still was a modest six and one-half dollars a day. By the late 1940s Gruber had been joined by a young bartender named Joe Miller, who later would become the owner.

Opposite page, top
The Paradise Inn was opened in 1946 by retired architect Robert Evans. This view shows the neatly landscaped grounds and the Spanish-style architecture of the resort, which was near the Jokake Inn off Camelback Road west of Scottsdale Road. Courtesy, Scottsdale Historical Society

Bottom
The Casa Blanca Inn, formerly the Donald Kellogg residence, was easily spotted because of its minaret domes on the roof. It operated as a resort for 30 years before it was converted into condominiums in the 1980s. Under the distinctive tower was a skylight opening into one portion of the original home. Courtesy, Scottsdale Historical Society

Following the war the community slowly got back on its feet. The Scottsdale Chamber of Commerce, first organized in 1921 but defunct since the Depression, was reactivated, and Wes Segner was named its first president. A community swimming pool, Sun Valley Pool, opened in 1948 near the high school on East Indian School Road. Admission was 35 cents for adults and 15 cents for children. Churches continued to flourish in the town with Mormons gathering at Scottsdale High School and Assembly of God members organizing as a congregation in the 1940s.

The year 1948 brought two great improvements. The first came when former newspaperman Lou Witzeman started the privately owned Rural Fire Department. "We started with one truck, one station and $27 in the bank," he said. The service later expanded to cover not only Scottsdale, but also other small communities in the east end of the valley. Witzeman became known for referring to owning the largest private fire protection department as "the same as having the world's largest square navel."

The second improvement was a town newspaper. Although Scottsdale had received a fair amount of coverage through the years in the Phoenix newspapers and had a few temporary news publications, including the *Scottsdale Journal* and *Scottsdale Booster,* it wasn't until 1948 that the weekly *Scottsdale Progress* came to town. It had begun in 1937 as the *Southside Progress,* based in and covering Tempe. It failed twice, however, in efforts to compete against the *Tempe Daily News,* which had been established in 1887. Francis Connolly, editor of the *TDN,* purchased the *Progress* and moved it to Scottsdale. The reborn newspaper printed its first issue on May 6, 1948, under editor James H. Boyd, who soon became the owner. The paper was sold again in 1959 to Victor J. Morgan and James G. Edmiston, who turned it into a daily on February 16, 1961. Jonathan Marshall bought the publication in 1963 and later purchased the Scottsdale-based weekly *Arizonian.*

More artists began to filter into town after the war. Novelist Glendon Swarthout left his native Michigan to settle in Scottsdale. He taught for a few years at Arizona State University, then began writing full time. *The Eagle and the Iron Cross* told of the German prisoners escaping from the Papago Park encampment. His *Cadillac Cowboys* was seen as a thinly veiled satire of the "nouveau riche" life in Scottsdale.

The art gallery scene that was to become Scottsdale's modern pride-and-joy had a slow and inauspicious start. Buck Saunders, a retired civil engineer and leisure-time painter from Virginia, had come to Arizona during the war. In 1949 he opened The Trading Post, an art supply store on Brown Street opposite Porter's Western Store. He traded art supplies for paintings and soon became an art dealer. Then he opened Buck Saunders Art Gallery. "In those first years, it was very hard to sell paintings, even though Scottsdale had some very fine artists. The winter people came in to get the native things. Painters were lucky to sell one painting."

Saunders began showing the pottery of Ted DeGrazia and soon staged his first exhibit of paintings. DeGrazia's first show with Saunders, February 5, 1950, attracted 1,500 viewers. The amazing turnout resulted from 50 invitations and a tiny advertisement in the weekly *Scottsdale Progress.* Among the guests were wealthy Maine Chance clients from the Elizabeth Arden beauty-care resort. They grabbed up DeGrazia watercolors, which then were selling for as little as $100. A month later Saunders gave a show for Pop Chalee, and Scottsdale's first art gallery was off and running.

When the Arizona Craft Center was destroyed by fire in 1950, the artists needed to find a new place to work. With the aid of Mrs. Fowler McCormick, Kiva New and Segner began building on two acres of an abandoned citrus orchard off Scottsdale Road, cutting a street (Fifth Avenue) through it to the west. Small storefronts were built and leased in September 1950 as the beginning of the street's now-famed shopping district. Kiva New built his own Kiva Craft Center around a pool and patio. "My idea," he said at the time, "is to establish an island to preserve the original theme of Scottsdale—crafts." One by one they came to set up easels and benches, potter's wheels, and weaving looms.

Among the first artisans in the Kiva Craft Center was Leona Caldwell, who created silk-screened fabric and fashions. Erne', the custom perfumer, joined soon after, creating fragrances for wealthy women and celebrities, Mamie Eisenhower and Eleanor Roosevelt among them. Alexander Kowal, the goldsmith, also set up a studio workshop in the village-within-a-village.

Segner also established the Craft Village on five acres located on the west side of Miller Road north of Indian School. He put up three concrete-block buildings for $17,000, one with discarded Coca-Cola signs as a roof. This was a working-artisans environment and included among its tenants glass artisan Joseph Maes, wood-carver Val Zaharek, and painter William Schimmel. Classes and exhibits were offered, and artists demonstrated their skills as prospective buyers looked on.

The town's artists' colony began to attract more visitors and Scottsdale, with a permanent population of only 2,000, soon became firmly established on the map as a tourist attraction. Mathilde Schaefer and Lew Davis moved out to Invergordon Road on Darlington property.

Mrs. McCormick, who, in the 1940s, had contributed to the arts culture by setting up Indian craftsmen on West Main Street, later

Opposite page, top
The McCormick Ranch home and stables stretch along Scottsdale Road in this 1947 aerial view. Indian Bend Road extends toward the upper left, and the Arizona Canal makes its turn at the Indian Bend Wash at upper right. A hotel now is on the site of the original buildings, and extensive housing development has occurred in the area to the north of the original townsite. Courtesy, Leonard Yuschik

Bottom
The Bank of Douglas was the forerunner of the Arizona Bank, located on Brown Avenue just south of Main Street. It was built by Malcolm White, who became the town's first mayor. The building still stands intact and in busy use by downtown businessmen and longtime residents who had their first accounts there. Courtesy, The Arizona Bank

built an Indian Center on her property west of Pima Road.

In 1947 Scottsdale businessmen had decided on the theme "The West's Most Western Town," and stores and other businesses began building fake Western fronts. Andy and Harriet Swick opened Swick's Clothing, a Western-wear store on Brown Avenue, joining Porter's of Arizona. About this time Lloyd Kiva decided to keep his shop open for the summer, as did several other merchants for the first time.

The town finally got its first movie house in June 1948, when Malcolm White opened the T-Bar-T Theater (now the Kiva Theater) on the south side of Main Street. He held a contest to name the theater, and Mrs. Frank Cavalliere won. White also built the Bank of Douglas on the southeast corner of Brown and Main streets. The bank was founded by Arizona mining entrepreneur Dr. James Douglas and was renamed the Arizona Bank in 1960.

Although the town had had electricity since 1920, it was not until 1949 that Central Arizona Light and Power Company (CALAPCO) provided Scottsdale with natural gas. This new convenience was part of a $90,000 project.

The school district had its ups and downs during this two-decade period. Early school board members, including William Messinger, Sr., and Warren Austin, had the planning foresight to buy acreage for the high school. For several years the school had a building on campus designated as Winfield Scott Junior High School, which was attended by seventh and eighth graders. In the late 1940s and early 1950s, the trustees also purchased 10-acre sites up and down the town's main agricultural laterals for $300 to $600 an acre. The idea was to have grade schools located two miles apart on half-mile roads because, as Messinger once said, "Nobody ever learned anything on a school bus."

The Goldwater merchandising family decided to expand outside Phoenix and opened a shop in 1950 on the east side of Scottsdale Road at First Avenue, now the site of Hobo Joe's. By this time the U.S. Census put Scottsdale's population at 2,032.

The town incorporation push was, a year later, prompted by the sale of a private water company to the City of Phoenix. This company had been owned by Merle Brown, former wife of E.E. "Brownie" Brown and daughter-in-law of E.O. Brown. Those who had a stake in the growing town realized the need for self-determination and filed petitions signed by landowners with the county. Incorporation was granted in June 1951 when Scottsdale consisted of 62 square miles of land and just over 2,000 people.

CHAPTER FOUR

Tourists and Townies

Three of the area's top movers and shakers take time out for some dress-up fun for an evening of partying: Tom Darlington, left, who encouraged and supported the Arizona Craftsmen Council; Robert Foehl, the resort operator who opened Lulu Belle's; and Ronald Byrnes, founder of several resorts including the Paradise Inn. Courtesy, City of Scottsdale

The move to incorporate was the small western town's first step toward becoming a sophisticated city and developing an image that would make it world-renowned within the next two decades. It already had a special ambience of art, resort life, and shops that made it more than just a suburb of Phoenix.

The push for incorporation was triggered by the Brown family's decision to sell its water company. Apparently no one in town wanted to buy it, so it was offered to the City of Phoenix. The resulting furor brought out in the open the previously privately discussed fear that Scottsdale might be annexed by Phoenix and consequently lose its individual identity; Tempe had incorporated earlier because of the same threat.

The decision to work for incorporation also was influenced by financial factors. If Scottsdale became part of Phoenix, residents would have to pay property taxes to that city. On the other hand, an incorporated community would be eligible for a share of state vehicle and gasoline taxes. Many residents had been complaining of inadequate fire and police protection, dusty streets, and poor street lighting. The town treasury had been a cigar box, and the street-sweeper was buying his own brooms after merchants collected funds to pay him.

Theater owner Malcolm White, however, was not convinced of the need for incorporation, an opinion supported by native George Thomas. But early in 1951, when White's T-Bar-T Theater was showing Abbott and Costello's *Little Giant,* the chamber of commerce initiated a door-to-door petition campaign headed by physician Philip H. Schneider and Cliff "Black Hat" Carpenter. Their goal was to obtain the signatures of more than two-thirds of approximately 400 tax-paying property owners from among some 1,200 persons residing in the area to be incorporated.

A counter petitioning effort, a last-ditch move to block incorporation by requiring an election to settle the question, was rejected by the Maricopa County board of supervisors on the basis that the pro-incorporation petitions had prior status. The board ruled for incorporation by a unanimous vote of 3-0 on June 25, 1951.

The board of supervisors appointed the first town council: farmer Bill Miller, CALAPCO manager Mort Kimsey, Saguaro Bar owner Jack Sweeney, blacksmith E.G. "Scotty" Scott, and White. A month later Miller resigned and George Cavalliere was his replacement. The council was expanded to seven members in March 1952 when two more residents—John Shoeman and V.D. Frederick—were appointed. The council remained exclusively male until 1958, when Mildred K. Bratzel was elected.

Despite the fact that Malcolm White had opposed incorporation, he was appointed as Scottsdale's first mayor. Later he was elected to two more terms and served until 1958. During the eight days following the election, the town council held three meetings to discuss garbage collection, dog control, sign protests, and off-street parking.

White recalled the arguments over one of the first orders of business—setting up a town fire district. The solution came when Lou Witzeman's Rural-Metro was contracted to serve Scottsdale. The six-year contract paid $4,260 a year. Witzeman had started the service in the late 1940s by going door-to-door to 1,000 homes asking if residents would pay $10 a year for fire protection. He took every dollar he collected and made a $900 down payment on a fire truck.

Malcolm White was an opponent of incorporation, but was appointed to the first town council and named Scottsdale's first mayor. It was his idea to use the Old West architectural theme in downtown Scottsdale. Courtesy, City of Scottsdale

Mayor White was designated as the first fire chief; Hurley Pruitt was named the first town marshal in September; Vergie Lutes (Mrs. Alvin) Brown became town clerk; and William Messinger was appointed the first town attorney.

At the time of incorporation, Scottsdale proper was a four-block downtown area. The town limits were Camelback, Thomas, and Miller roads and the Arizona Canal. Among the businesses were Earl's Market, Porter's Western Wear, Saba's Department Store, Scottsdale Hardware (soon to become Paul's Hardware), Scottsdale Service Company, Willmoth Appliance, Swick's Clothing Store, Goldwaters Desert Fashions, Hanny's, Scottsdale Motors, Lute's Pharmacy, Scotty's Blacksmith Shop, McGee's Indian Den, the Bank of Douglas, and the Tico Taco Mexican Restaurant.

Brown Avenue still was not completely paved, with the south end only a dirt road in front of the Catholic church and Cavalliere's. There still was an abundance of undeveloped land at Scottsdale and Camelback roads, with a rodeo and horse-show grounds located on the northwest corner acreage. This land later became Fashion Square with the building of a large Goldwaters store in 1961. The decade of the 1950s, under the auspices of new town government, was to yield many changes that would set Scottsdale apart from its neighboring communities.

A group of movers and shakers known as The Mag's Ham Bun Bunch organized in 1953 as a coterie of downtown businessmen. They first met every weekday morning at Lute's for a half-hour of

Left
The city's original seal, depicting a cowboy on a bucking bronco, epitomizes Scottsdale's reputation as "The West's Most Western Town." The seal was designed in 1951, upon the city's incorporation, by Mrs. Gene Brown Pennington, granddaughter of E.O. Brown, an early town power. Courtesy, City of Scottsdale

Below
The earliest Arabian horse shows in Scottsdale were staged at the rodeo arena at the northwest corner of Scottsdale and Camelback roads, now the site of Fashion Square. Courtesy, Bob Petley

Above
Lou Witzeman's Rural Metro Fire Department stands in front of the city hall/fire station in 1951. The building was located at the northwest corner of Brown and Second streets. Courtesy, City of Scottsdale

THE CHAMBER OF COMMERCE OF SCOTTSDALE
Cordially Invites Everybody in Arizona!
THE FIRST ANNUAL
SCOTTSDALE SUNSHINE
Saturday
Nov. 17th
Festival
OPENING WINTER SEASON 1951-1952
MAIN STREET • SCOTTSDALE, ARIZONA
SATURDAY, NOVEMBER 17
COLORFUL PARADE
STARTS AT 3P.M.
30 MINUTES OF
REAL WESTERN
ENTERTAINMENT
DICK GRIFFITH
FREE to the PUBLIC
THE MARIACHES
MEXICAN STREET SINGERS
The Western Way in the
"West's Most Western Town"
BIG BARBECUE 5 p. m.
in front of AMERICAN LEGION BUILDING
From 5 to 7 p.m. — $1.50 per Heaped Plate
Sponsored and served by members of the American
Legion of Scottsdale. Real Western Food prepared in
the real western way . . . and plenty of it.
STREET DANCE 7 p. m.
and CONTINUING UNTIL THE WEE SMA' HOURS
Music by JOE ARONSON
and his WESTERN TYPE ORCHESTRA
EVERYTHING FREE But the Barbecue!
All Kinds of Dancing • for All Kinds of People
SQUARE DANCING • ROUND DANCING • WALTZ • POLKA
Both MODERN and OLD WESTERN
This invitation to visit the "West's Most Western Town" is sponsored by:
Goldwater's • Henry's • Leonards • McDougall - Cassou • O'Malley Lumber Co. • Porters • Clay Smith

Opposite page, left
The Scottsdale Sunshine Festival opened the winter season of 1951-1952 with a parade, barbecue dinner for $1.50, western entertainment, mariachis, and a street dance in the evening. Courtesy, Scottsdale Daily Progress

Right, top
The original Sunshine Festival was marked by the giant-sized cowboy sign that still stands in downtown Scottsdale. This simple beginning of a 20-minute parade has grown into the Parada del Sol, a chamber of commerce event held in February each year during the height of the tourist season. It is ranked in the top 10 of nationwide events of its kind. Courtesy, Buck Saunders

Right, bottom
Earl Shipp (left) and Lute Wasbotten (right) were among the town's early movers and shakers. Wasbotten was a member of the city council from 1954-1958. Courtesy, Thelma Steiner Holveck

coffee and conversation and later moved to the larger Mag's restaurant. Charter member Earl Shipp recalled that no one was allowed to join until he bought coffee for the house.

Scottsdale's Mexican population made its own contribution to the town's ever-burgeoning cultural scene. A pageant called "The Miracle of the Roses" had begun in 1949 with the Gonzales brothers standing on the steps of the Little Red Schoolhouse and singing their ballad to Our Lady of Guadalupe. This evolved into a simple presentation on a flatbed truck in the Mexican barrio, and then into an outdoor pageant with a candlelit procession. This event attracted members of the community and tourists for many years. It was directed during the 1950s and 1960s by artist Paul Coze from a script written by poet Patricia Benton. Jesus Corral provided assistance in the production.

The Scottsdale Community Players organized in 1952 as an all-volunteer little theater group. Although the group survived for years in humble shelters, it finally raised enough funds to build its 200-seat Stagebrush Theater.

Scottsdale's now world-famous Parada del Sol rodeo and parade also had its simple beginning during this era. The winter season officially opened on November 17, 1951, with an event known as the Sunshine Festival. Its early format was a 20 minute parade of perhaps 20 entries, a public barbecue dinner, and street dance. Scottsdale's original self-described "drugstore cowboy," Lute Wasbotten, was the marshal of the first parade and chairman of the second festival. Wasbotten recalled that "it wasn't much of a parade"—no floats, just the Scottsdale High School Beaver Band led by faculty member Eugene Hanson, another band from Williams Air Force Base, some riders, and mariachis to entertain the crowd until the parade began. The barbecue dinner, held in the American Legion hall, cost one dollar and fifty cents a plate; 8,000 people showed up, but the food ran out. The Scottsdale Jaycees, organized in 1953, took over the festival that year and changed its name to Parada del Sol (Spanish for "parade in the sun"). To make it available to more tourists they moved it to mid-season. The Parada del Sol soon earned the distinction of being "the world's longest horse-drawn parade" because no motorized floats were permitted. Rodeo events and weekend Western mock gunfights were added in 1956. Then, in 1958, the Hashknife Gang (members of the Navajo County Sheriff's Posse) began making a grueling 200-mile pony-express ride with relay riders carrying a load of specially postmarked mail over the mountains from Holbrook to Scottsdale.

A new breed of health-seekers came to town when Elizabeth Arden established her Maine Chance getaway spot in the 1950s. She bought a 45-acre estate with cottages and two swimming pools on the south slope of Camelback Mountain and set up her winter staff there. Entertainment stars and notables including Perle Mesta, Clare Boothe Luce, Mary Pickford, Ava Gardner, and Edna Ferber came from around the nation and the world.

Scottsdale's reputation for arts, crafts, and specialty shops gained momentum too. Ruth Sussman had come from the School of American Ballet in New York City to open a modern school of classical ballet. Italian architect Paolo Soleri, formerly a protege of Frank Lloyd Wright, established Cosanti, a complex of earth-formed concrete structures in an area north of the city. It became the site of drafting studios, craft workshops, living areas, and display space. It was here that the now world-famous Soleri bronze windbells and sculptures were created. Later Soleri established Arcosanti, his energy-efficient dream city of the future, in the desert highlands farther to the north.

In 1959 Louise Lincoln Kerr, daughter of the Cleveland, Ohio, industrialist who founded Camelback Inn, built an adobe chamber music studio-home on 20 acres of desert north of the city. It still is in use today.

With the accent on tourists playing cowboy, David Saba, Sr., had expanded his Chandler clothing store business in 1947 to take over the former drugstore at the northwest corner of Brown and Main. In 1950 a second Saba's store was opened up the street with the family business eventually involving his five sons: Roger, Norman, David, Jr., Edward, and Richard. A branch store of Porter's, one of the state's oldest western-wear firms, had a thriving business going in the two-story old post office building around the corner on Brown. Later, former saddle-maker Bob Meadows and his wife, Margie, bought the store from the Porter family. But other tastes were catered to as well. The Craig House, a store for gentlemen run by the Morton family of salt fame, carried English tweeds, cashmere sweaters, and $900 sports jackets made from the wool of the rare Andes vicuna.

The Fifth Avenue area continued to develop under Lloyd Kiva New's direction as did a downtown mixture of shops, including Christine Rae's, with its silk-screened fabrics and squaw dresses, and the Jon Bonnells' White Hogan, where Navajo silversmiths worked as customers watched. Brice and Judy Sewell established Indian Arts on Fifth Avenue, where they were joined by Paul Huldermann and his House of Six Directions.

In 1952 Buck Saunders opened a second gallery on Scottsdale Road south of Thomas, but also continued to operate his original shop on Brown Avenue until 1972. William O'Brien of Chicago opened O'Brien's Art Emporium on Sixth Avenue on December 26, 1956.

Opposite page, top
Spring training of professional baseball teams began attracting tourists in the mid-1950s when the Baltimore Orioles flew into their "winter nest" to get ready for the season. Stadium seats afford a view of Camelback Mountain to the west. Courtesy, City of Scottsdale

Bottom
The Louise Lincoln Kerr Center is a gathering place for those appreciative of arts and crafts. Initially the home of its namesake, the house has been refurbished and strengthened though its rustic facade has been preserved. Photo by Suzanne Starr/Scottsdale Daily Progress

National figures came to Scottsdale in the 1950s to visit the G. Robert Herbergers, who had built a home at the southeast corner of MacDonald Drive and Scottsdale Road when they moved from Minnesota. Guests for their Saturday night dance club included Hubert and Muriel Humphrey and the exiled Prince of Lichtenstein. The widowed Eleanor Roosevelt, in the valley to visit her daughter, Anna, often browsed in Scottsdale's unusual shops. The accounts of these peripatetic experiences in her nationally syndicated column, "My Day," helped bring fame and recognition to the city. Soon the little town that had begun with one main crossroads (waggishly referred to by those from big-city Phoenix as "Stopsdale") was becoming known as "Shopsdale."

Scottsdale also was gaining a reputation as a dude-ranch center, with these added to the scene: Flying T Ranch and Rancho Vista Bonita in 1951; The Bunk House, Sun Down Ranch, and Yellow Boot Ranch in 1952; and Sundial Guest Ranch, Paradise Valley Guest Ranch, and Turquoise Ranch in 1953. More major hotels began springing up—the Valley Ho, Safari, and Executive House within a one-square-mile area—marking the start of the city's real growth as a center for tourism.

Major league baseball spring training camps enhanced the Scottsdale tourist scene starting in 1955 with the Baltimore Orioles flying to their "winter nest" in the new city stadium with its spectacular view of Camelback Mountain to the west. The Boston Red Sox took over in the late 1950s, and other major league teams came in succeeding years.

Tourism was further boosted by the winter of 1957, which was a miserable one in Florida. That turned out to be a benefit for Scottsdale because many southeastern tourists came to Arizona instead and discovered its many resorts. They returned as perennial visitors. Among their discoveries was the Royal Palms Inn with its Mediterranean-style central building, which was the former home of the Travis family of Greyhound Bus fame, and later the Cook Travel Agency family. Its owner, Charles Alberding, had taken over the Paradise Inn in 1950 and the Jokake Inn in 1951. Royal Palms Inn manager Pat Ryan, previously Alberding's secretary, recalled that on the night of the announcement of purchase, guests from both resorts went out and tore down the fence between the two. Among the perennial Royal Palms guests in the 1950s was physician-cartoonist Nick Dalis. He created comic strips including "Rex Morgan M.D.," "Judge Parker," and "Apt. 3D" and later became a permanent resident of Scottsdale. Owner Alberding also was one of the behind-the-scenes forces, along with Jack Stewart, in the founding of the Fiesta Bowl to promote tourism during December.

In 1952, 67 building permits were issued in Scottsdale with a total valuation of $566,150. More and more old and new businesses were picking up on White's idea of an Old West downtown theme. By August 1958 the Old Town businessmen formally had agreed to maintain the Dodge City western architecture style. The former Farmers' State Bank building had been purchased in the early 1950s by Flo and "Sparky" Sparks, who turned it into a tavern called The Rusty Spur. They converted the vault to liquor storage and office space. In 1951 E.O. Brown's store, formerly the Craft Center, became the Posie Post florist shop.

A March 12, 1956, *Life* magazine article contributed to Scottsdale's boom by calling the town one of the most desirable communities in the West. The article said, "None has such conspicuous glitter as the gold-plated town of Scottsdale, Arizona."

By now Scottsdale was emerging from its cocoon as a beautiful butterfly in a paradise setting of golf courses, dude ranches, and resorts. There were date and citrus groves, quiet desert trails, and even more celebrity residents, including author Clarence Buddington Kelland.

The electronics industry also was attracted by the town's new image. In 1957 Motorola, Inc., established its Military Electronics Division for aerospace technology (renamed the Government Electronics Division in 1966). The division, which helped put the first man on the moon, opened at 8201 E. McDowell Road with 1,250 employees, most of whom became residents of Scottsdale. The firm had come to Arizona in 1949 due to the foresight of Daniel E. Noble, who set up a laboratory in rented space in Phoenix, followed by a plant the company opened on 56th Street in 1950 and the Semiconductor Products Division built at 5005 East McDowell Road in 1956.

In 1951 Scottsdale High School graduated 57 students, and four years later there were four elementary schools. By 1960 nine more schools had been added, including Arcadia High.

The Scottsdale Boys Club, organized in 1954, offered activities at Scottsdale Grammar School. With the help of the Scottsdale Coordinating Committee, a group of civic-minded residents working together for community betterment, a building site was secured at Osborn and Hinton (now 75th Street). Architect Joe Wong donated his services, and the first permanent clubhouse was dedicated in 1959. A Girls Club was founded in 1960 through efforts of the Civitan Club and expanded in 1978 with a northern branch.

The face of the town gradually became more sophisticated. As the restaurant scene began to develop in 1952, native-born rancher George Thomas drove his last herd of cattle down Scottsdale Road.

The original Winfield Scott home was torn down, and Bimbo's Restaurant was built. Unfortunately, the chaplain's beloved shade trees ringing the property at the northeast corner of Scottsdale and Indian School roads were chopped down to make way for a parking lot.

Robert Foehl, former manager of Jokake Inn and owner of the Valley Ho Hotel, bought the old Kubelsky-Boston Store location as a wedding gift to his bride. For several years it had been the Saguaro Bar, a local cowboy hangout known for Saturday night bar fights that spilled out into Main Street. In 1954 Foehl and his wife turned the place into Lulu Belle's, Scottsdale's first really posh restaurant, and he hired Buzz Dublin as manager. One of Lulu Belle's later managers, Dale Anderson, became a noted restaurateur in his own right.

During this period the commercial side of Scottsdale grew rather slowly. In 1952 most of the 70 businesses closed during the off-season, but by 1954, 284 firms stayed open year-round. In 1956 the city had 11 restaurants, five art galleries, 10 gift shops, two automobile agencies, and one trailer park. Another bank, Western Savings and Loan, came into the community in 1957.

Soon more and more tourists came to taste the relaxed simplicity of western living, riding desert trails and supping around chuckwagon fires. They seemed to like the Hollywoodesque Old West style of the town. Jim Frederick's Chevron station became "Frederick's Auto and Livery Stable" to fit in with the claim that Scottsdale was "The West's Most Western Town." Visitors were entranced by stores with knotty pine facades, rustic signs, western names, and hitching rails out front. Amid the shiny station wagons with out-of-state plates, Indians in horse-drawn wagons still came from the reservation on Saturdays, and locals often rode into the town that claimed "Horses have the right of way."

In 1958 Jack Huntress converted the Western Auto repair store (formerly the site of Scotty's Blacksmith Shop on Scottsdale Road at First Avenue) into a soda fountain-luncheonette that he called The Sugar Bowl. The F.W. Woolworth Company built an 1890s-style two-story building on the northwest corner of Scottsdale Road and Main Street. But the town was not big enough to support the department store, so after a few years it became The Wigwam, and since then only the ground floor has been open. Al Thies, who came from Chicago to open a bakery on Indian School Road, soon became the pet of visiting celebrities. They included Jackie Gleason, Arthur Murray, and Phil Harris. One of his most famous creations was a three-tiered wedding cake for Natalie Wood and Robert Wagner, who were married in 1961 across the street at the Valley Ho.

Right
Chaplain Scott's carefully nurtured citrus and olive trees were cut down to make room for the parking lot of Bimbo's restaurant in the 1950s. This 1957 photo shows the intersection of Scottsdale and Indian School roads, with the Bashas' grocery store at lower left, a gas station toward the center, and the Ranch House hamburger stand toward the bottom. Scottsdale High School is at the upper edge of the photo, and the First Baptist Church of Scottsdale is shown still standing at center right. Courtesy, City of Scottsdale

Left
Lulu Belle's Restaurant had a Gay '90s theme when it opened in 1954 as Scottsdale's first really posh eatery. Its red-and-white batten-board siding still makes it a landmark near Scottsdale and Main. When this advertisement appeared in a local publication around 1958, "Buzz" and Mary Helen Dublin were running the place. Courtesy, City of Scottsdale

Several non-western, decidedly continental businesses also thrived in this movie-set town: Louis Germaine started his classy French restaurant, Chez Louis, on the east side of Brown Avenue north of Main Street, where dinner prices ranged from $2.95 to $4.95. Trader Vic's opened on Fifth Avenue, and French-born Etienne Gluck established his gourmet restaurant on Stetson Drive. Other French restaurants, including Pierre le Coz's Le Bistro and Daniel Huon's La Chaumiere, joined the others downtown in 1969.

Paul Shank, a Mennonite farm boy from Pennsylvania who had gained cooking experience in the Wyoming oil fields during the Depression, opened Paul Shank's Fine Dining at the Safari Hotel and Resort in 1959. The Safari had opened three years earlier on Scottsdale Road north of Camelback. The former Thomas Riley Marshall home became a tearoom, The Shutters, and later a tavern, Der Steiner. And the Safari Hotel's French Quarter booked top-name acts, including the DeCastro Sisters, Dennis Day, The Modernaires, the Four Freshmen, Rosemary Clooney, the Ink Spots, and Tiny Tim. The adjunct coffee shop was one of the few eateries in town open after-hours, catering to the late-night appetites of both locals and visiting celebrities.

In 1958 Mayor White, who had served three terms, finally declined another. While he was in office, the town's population had increased to 4,000, and its land area had expanded five times. The town offices had been relocated to the Little Red Schoolhouse after the building was purchased in 1955 by millionaire Walker McCune. White's logical successor in office was Mort Kimsey, a resident since 1917. Kimsey continued to work to promote and preserve the community's western flavor during his term of office from 1958-1962.

Mildred Crosier, the town's first full-time employee, had been hired as an accountant in 1958 for $75 a week. The budget was tight under Gordon Allison, who served as the first city manager for $150 a week, so Crosier always used both sides of adding machine tapes. Once when she ran out of usable tape, she made a graphic point by substituting bathroom tissue. "We didn't have any money for supplies, and very little to operate on, but they got me some tape the next day," she said.

A protracted round of annexation battles with Phoenix began in the 1950s. In round one Scottsdale lost the high-income Arcadia area and Camelback Mountain, but in later bouts retained the area south of town to the county line. The peace pipe finally was accepted by both parties through deannexation agreements.

Religious activity continued to expand with the Episcopalians organizing in October 1953 at the home of Guy Stillman. The first services were held the next month in the Scottsdale High School cafeteria. The Christian Scientists had their first services the same year. First Baptist, the original church in town, moved into a new building on Osborn Road in 1957. Scottsdale Presbyterian Church organized in 1958, with its services first held in the American Legion Hall, then the Kiva Theater (formerly the T-Bar-T), then the Masonic Hall until its permanent building was completed in 1960 at Hayden and Osborn roads.

William Messinger's sons became involved in city life and business before the decade was out. Philip served as city attorney for several years and Paul opened Messinger Mortuary in 1959. He later served in the city council and the state legislature.

Paul Messinger recalled school district problems caused by federal desegregation requirements in the 1950s. They brought about the closing of the Little Red Schoolhouse (Coronado School) despite local officials' protests that it qualified to remain open under the separate but equal provision. "Some of the Mexican students floundered after that, because they didn't have the chance to learn English in the early grades," he said.

By 1960 census data put Scottsdale's population at 10,026 in a land area covering 3.8 square miles. The town, at the brink of its secondary development, stretched toward city status.

Mort Kimsey, Scottsdale's second mayor and charter member of the town council, lived 57 years in the community. He was a government entomologist and managed Central Arizona Light and Power Company (Calapco), founded by his father William and later purchased by Arizona Public Service. Kimsey also operated a garage and service station at Scottsdale and Main from 1919 to 1945. He was a familiar figure on the downtown streets, once described as a "tall, lanky cuss with graying brown hair and a droopy Wyatt Earp mustache." Courtesy, City of Scottsdale

CHAPTER FIVE

Jewel in the Desert

This aerial view of Scottsdale was taken by photographer Bob Petley in the late 1970s. Scottsdale Memorial Hospital is in the lower center portion of the photo. Courtesy, Bob Petley

The decade of the 1960s was a time of directed growth for Scottsdale, a decade in which the town emerged from its early rough-ore state to take on the glowing richness of Arizona's native turquoise to become a jewel in the desert. The transition did not happen quickly or smoothly however.

The kick-off year, 1961, was a big one. Governor Paul Fannin signed the town's charter, which established a mayor-council-manager form of government, and then on October 16, 1961, a city charter was signed. Scottsdale had officially graduated from town to city status with an initial budget of $2.2 million.

The population influx between 1956 and 1964 caused school enrollment to soar. Old-timers had scoffed at such predictions, but the increased population required the building of eight schools in this eight-year period, including Coronado and Saguaro high schools in 1961 and 1966.

During this period, Scottsdale was a city with two very separate populations—tourists attracted by the charm of arts, crafts, and resorts and year-round homeowners seeking escape from the stress of urban confinement.

Municipal missteps and deannexation battles clouded Scottsdale's growth in the 1960s. The result was the city's most severe growing pains, including internal scandals and a succession of four city managers in as many years. In 1962 Kimsey was succeeded in the mayor's seat by rancher Bill Schrader, who served one term until 1964. Schrader was followed in office in March 1964 by John Woudenberg, a former professional football player. During the beginning of Woudenberg's term, the county attorney began investigating charges of a police and city scandal. Newspaper headlines reported "Three Cops Fired After Theft Probe" and "City Till Tap Charged." Six months after he was sworn in, Woudenberg resigned, pleading "pressure of business," although his decision was not believed to be linked with either of those scandals.

The next three mayors were appointed, rather than elected, to their first terms. The city council chose one of its members, building contractor Bill Clayton, to succeed Woudenberg as mayor. Clayton inherited the problems of another annexation dispute that involved the city's east side. The Arizona Supreme Court ruled that the 1961 annexation of the six-square-mile area and its 25,000

Opposite page, top
Howdy Dudettes greeted tourists beginning in the late 1950s. Courtesy, Scottsdale Chamber of Commerce

Bottom left
William Schrader was mayor from 1962 to 1964. Courtesy, City of Scottsdale

Bottom right
John Woudenberg was mayor for six turbulent months in 1964. Courtesy, City of Scottsdale

Above
In 1962 Scottsdale was growing, but the land to the north of the center of town was still open in many areas. Courtesy, Thelma Steiner Holveck

Right
William Clayton, Scottsdale's fifth mayor, rallied citizen support for annexations through community involvement committees that developed a general plan for development. Courtesy, City of Scottsdale

Jonathan Marshall, publisher-editor of the Scottsdale Daily Progress, *remembers Scottsdale as a relaxed little community of the early 1960s. Courtesy, Scottsdale Daily Progress*

residents was illegal because there were not enough signatures from property owners. Thus the area was scheduled to revert to the county, causing the loss of past and future tax monies. But during the 15 days before the ruling took effect, city employees and supportive citizens began circulating new petitions among homeowners and succeeded in gaining enough signatures to put the area back into the city.

The community now was being served by two newspapers, the weekly *Arizonian* and the *Scottsdale Progress,* which had become a daily in 1961 with a circulation of less than 2,000. Jonathan Marshall bought the newspaper in 1963 with a circulation of 4,800 that went to 7,500 by 1966, and continued an upward spiral as the city grew. Under Marshall's direction, the newspaper editorialized for responsible government, city beautification, a strong sign ordinance, a master plan, strict zoning enforcement, a civic center complex, and more park land. By now the city also had its own radio station, first using the call letters KWBY and later changing to KDOT, KSGR, and finally KOPA.

In 1963, in a huge leap from the 1956 tally, there were 259 hotel rooms, 14 art galleries, 51 gift shops, and 56 restaurants. But the blossoming business climate was withering on the edges.

A *Progress* editorial in 1964 pinpointed the young city's weaknesses as "lack of community pride, inadequate planning, and the need to foster a healthy economy." Clayton had inherited this situation during his year in office and was running for reelection when he died of a heart attack in late 1965. During that one year, however, he had recognized the need for action and sought a way to get the residents involved in the future of their city. That way, proposed by City Manager Richard Malcolm, was the Scottsdale Town Enrichment Program (STEP). It began as a coalition of 80 city voters meeting with 20 elected officials and city staff members to study the city's needs. Later it expanded to 14 groups from elementary school attendance areas. Topics of study, which were pinpointed by seven task force committees, involved marathon discussion sessions totaling 2,000 hours. The result was a listing of long-range and short-range goals for the city, which focused on both private and public land use and on the development of utilities, transportation, and an economic and tax base.

The city's General Plan became a guide for its physical development, including plans for a street network, proposed park and school locations, and types of uses for various land areas. It designated locations for apartments and resorts, shopping centers, and industrial areas, as well as establishing residential densities. Five-year priorities included an airport, expanded library facilities, land for parks and recreation, a civic center, and a plan to attract garden-type industrial plants. All these goals were attained, due in part to the hiring in 1963 of the city's first planning director, George Fretz. Voters backed the plan by approving a parks bond issue in 1965 when the city had only one tiny park, which was located near the downtown municipal swimming pool. A $22 million flood-control bond issue was approved in 1966, followed by another approving funds for a civic center.

City officials were determined to regulate the community's ambience in other ways. Among the ordinances passed was one in 1962 prohibiting the erection of new billboards. This was a forerunner to the 1969 sign-control ordinance that regulated the placement and size of new signs. Its passage resulted in a group of merchants temporarily splitting from the chamber of commerce in protest.

After Clayton's death the third draft choice for mayor came out of the council, young optometrist Bud Tims. The following February, instead of running for council reelection, he became a successful write-in candidate for mayor. Tims, aided by City Manager Bill Donaldson, immediately took up where Clayton left off, further encouraging the activity of the STEP committees and expanding their numbers and responsibilities. Tims was returned to office in 1968 and 1972 before resigning in 1974 to make a successful bid for the Arizona Corporation Commission, where he served until his death in 1983.

Another major decision was made in the 1960s that would bring national recognition to Scottsdale. Geographically, the city is divided from east to west by the Indian Bend Wash, a narrow stretch of land seven and one-half miles long that covers 1,227 acres. It was usually a dry stream bed, but it also had caused havoc since the early days of the community. There were 15 ravaging floods in a half-century of flow from Indian Bend Road south to McKellips Road. In 1965 Congress authorized the Army Corps of Engineers to study drainage and urban flood control problems in Maricopa County and to work out a solution. First priority was given to the Indian Bend Wash. A concrete-lined channel was proposed to carry the flood runoff from the Arizona Canal to the Salt River bed to the south. A county-wide citizens' committee was formed in 1966 and a bond proposal to finance the construction was put on the ballot. It failed, particularly in Scottsdale, because residents resisted the idea of such an ugly solution to the flooding problem. Concrete, they said, might be economical, strong, lasting, and effective, but it would be both a physical and psychological barrier within the community. So the plan was scrapped.

B.L. "Bud" Tims served as the city's sixth mayor and further encouraged citizen involvement in Scottsdale's growth. During his tenure the Indian Bend Wash park system was begun, and the civic center complex took shape. Courtesy, City of Scottsdale

Above
A 1965 aerial view of the intersection of Indian School and Hayden roads looking west shows an engulfed service station in the center and a shopping center parking lot a bit drier to the left as the Indian Bend Wash flows following heavy rainfall. Courtesy, Scottsdale Daily Progress

Left
Osborn Road, one of the major east-west streets in Scottsdale, was a raging flood in 1968. This view, looking east toward Scottsdale Presbyterian Church on Hayden Road, demonstrates how severely the community was divided during flooding season in the late winter. The Indian Bend Wash development provided for side drains to divert the waters and for a grassy channel to confine the flooding. Courtesy, Scottsdale Daily Progress

Architect Bennie Gonzales designed Scottsdale's civic center complex, including its city hall, library, and arts center, with fountains, pools, and a grassy walking mall. Courtesy, City of Scottsdale

Several alternatives were proposed, however, and the idea of a greenbelt or turf channel was discussed. It would be planted with trees and shrubs and serve as reservoir areas for water storage during flood periods. The greenbelt would confine floodwaters to their natural path of flow through the construction of inlets and outlets, side drains, and levees. It was a dual-purpose plan that would disturb fewer homes and be far more aesthetic. The proposal went through various phases, and work finally got under way after agreements came from all involved—the city, Corps of Engineers, and federal government—as well as private developers, who wanted to build golf courses on the greenbelt.
In 1973 Scottsdale voters authorized a $10 million bond issue to fund the city's portion of the development, and the U.S. Army Corps of Engineers committed some $15 million to the project, supplemented by county funds. What once was a wandering flood plain and a city liability would be transformed into a scenic grassy area of park land within walking distance of more than 60,000 people. It was a successful transition that would take another decade to accomplish. Scottsdale's recovery from its internal problems, accompanied by its decisive steps forward, brought it a nomination in 1967 for an All America City award.

One other important civic need as pinpointed by the STEP committee was a civic center. Local architect Bennie Gonzales was hired to design the complex, which included a city hall, library, and arts center with walking mall. Two bond elections were passed to provide $2.4 million in funds for the complex and to develop a parks system. The civic center's 14-acre site (six city blocks) was separated from the main part of the downtown shopping area by a deteriorating blighted area. The site was chosen deliberately to encourage urban renewal in the area. But due to small lot sizes, multiple ownerships, and high land costs, the plan failed.

The city then sought federal redevelopment funds for the 20-acre downtown area and an 18-acre slum known as Vista del Camino in the Indian Bend Wash floodplain. Many of the downtown houses were Mexican adobe huts that were deteriorating. The Vista residents were the Yaqui Indian families, descendants of refugees from the Mexican Revolution, living in substandard housing. The Neighborhood Development Program aimed at providing housing near original residences while upgrading the area. A $9 million federal grant with matching city funds and in-kind services carried out the project.

The redevelopment included the Scottsdale Mall, Scottsdale Center for the Arts, hotel-convention center (Doubletree Corp.), restaurants, shops, offices, a parking garage, and a police-city court complex, all completed by the mid-1970s. The city hall landscape was enhanced by sculptures, fountains, and pools. The result pleased townies and attracted tourists.

The future of the Little Red Schoolhouse looked bleak after it lost city hall and the library to the new civic complex. But the venerable building was spared from a wrecker's ball after the Scottsdale Historical Society was organized expressly to save it in mid-1968. A fund raising goal of $60,000 was announced to repair the building so it would remain usable. The campaign, led by former school lunch program head Clara Beauchamp and former Mayor Mort Kimsey, touched the hearts and wallets of businessmen, merchants, and residents alike. Many stores set aside a percentage of their profits to donate to the cause, and schoolchildren began a mile-of-pennies drive. Donated renovating materials were pledged, and 1,000 miniature school slates were sold by the Scottsdale Historical Society in cooperation with the chamber of commerce. Four years later, in November 1972, a Little Red Schoolhouse Ball was held in celebration of the successful campaign, and an important bit of Scottsdale Americana was preserved as the city council awarded the chamber of commerce a 25-year lease for one dollar a year.

Members of the Scottsdale Chamber of Commerce had organized the Scottsdale Charros in 1961 as a special organization to help promote events to benefit the city. *Charros* translates from Spanish as "gentleman riders," and its members go on an annual trail ride complete with haute cuisine. Through the years they have been instrumental in attracting professional baseball clubs for spring training: the Chicago Cubs, 1964 to 1978; the Oakland Athletics, 1979 to 1981; and the San Francisco Giants, starting in 1982. The Charros also sponsor the Fiesta Bowl marathon run, professional golf championships, tennis tournaments, and have cosponsored the All-Arabian Horse Show.

Jim Palmer, who became a pitcher for Baltimore, was a Scottsdale High School graduate, and fellow Oriole hurler Steve Stone established Steven Restaurant in the downtown area. Other professional baseball players who settled in and around Scottsdale include Rick Monday, Carl Hubbell, Bobbie Adams, and Joe Garagiola.

Country-western music star Waylon Jennings gained his first recognition in the early 1960s performing at Wild Bill's (later the Handelbar J). Another show business success who first tried out his talents in Scottsdale was film producer Steven Spielberg, while an Arcadia High School student.

As noted in a Valley National Bank advertisement in the *Scottsdale Daily Progress* on June 25, 1966 (the 15th anniversary of the city's incorporation), Scottsdale had much to be proud of: the first Arizona city to establish a comprehensive land use study, to require underground utility lines, to have designed and proposed to voters a total civic center plan, to have a downtown design plan, and to have a park system assisted by returned federal tax funds. More and more Phoenix residents were coming to Scottsdale, including business and professional men such as stockbrokers, who wanted to be closer to their clients.

By the late 1960s Scottsdale was becoming well known for its park facilities, which included man-made lakes stocked with fish and inhabited by ducks. Water was pumped from the lakes and used to irrigate the landscaping. Eldorado Park, completed in 1968, was heralded as the nation's first urban campground, with pull-in pads for vehicles.

There was, however, one area in which Scottsdale had made little progress: the town did not have a hospital. In 1962 private investors offered bonds paying eight percent, a high rate at the time. They raised about $1.2 million. City Hospital of Scottsdale, a one-story 120-bed facility, was built in the heart of the old town area for $90,000. The investors reportedly pocketed the rest of the money. The building was poorly constructed, with doorknobs literally coming off in staff members' hands.

In addition to shoddy construction, the hospital suffered from poor management. It was so bad that the medical staff, which had its first organizational meeting in the back room of the Red Dog Saloon, refused to use the facility. "We agreed to admit no more patients until some changes were made," said Robert C. Foreman, M.D., a surgeon who retired from the staff in 1982. "After about a week, the hospital's board of trustees resigned, the medical staff reorganized and a new board was appointed." But the hospital's instability continued to be evident and admissions decreased alarmingly as people opted for treatment in Phoenix or Mesa. "We even had time to play cards or games with the patients to relieve our boredom and theirs," said Nurse Pat Sampair. At one point there was only one patient in the building.

Finally, in 1964, the Southern Baptist Convention of Arizona took over the hospital and renamed it Baptist Hospital of Scottsdale. It soon gained an improved reputation and, in 1968, the first in a series of expansions and improvements was begun. More land was purchased, and a two-story addition went up. A year later four more stories were added to make a six-story tower that opened in April 1970 and provided 232 beds and five specialized medical departments. In 1971 the hospital was chartered and turned over to the community to be run as a nonprofit community facility. It was renamed Scottsdale Memorial Hospital.

Also in 1964, the city formed a nonprofit municipal corporation

Jim Palmer, a Scottsdale High School graduate and Baltimore Orioles pitcher, was among the spring training players who came to Scottsdale. Courtesy, Scottsdale Daily Progress

Opposite page, top
In 1977 Scottsdale Municipal Airport still was a small facility, but was soon developed with an industrial park and the center of nearly 300 businesses by the early 1980s. Courtesy, City of Scottsdale

Bottom
Two generations of Indian artists were together in the late 1960s at the Scottsdale National Indian Arts Exhibition. From left are Alfred Kee Gorman, his father Carl N. Gorman (looking at his painting, Bustles and Bells), *R.C. Gorman of San Francisco with Mrs. Carl N. Gorman and her daughter Zonnie. Courtesy, Scottsdale Historical Society*

aided by federal funds to take over 200 acres of Thunderbird Field from the Seventh-Day Adventist Conference. The conference wanted to donate the land to the city, but could not legally do so. Therefore, the city bought the land, and the conference gave the $750,000 back to the city as a gift.

Soon the $2 million Scottsdale Municipal Airport was developed with the adjacent Scottsdale Industrial Air Park and branch fire station. Because the Central Arizona Project had a major aqueduct running through the area, a large recreational park and residential subdivisions with helipads and individual taxi ways to the lots were envisioned. The vision became reality as firms began to locate in the area. By the early 1980s it would become a center of nearly 300 businesses with more than 2,700 employees.

Garbage, of all things, also put Scottsdale on the national map in the 1960s. The city developed the nation's first completely mechanized fleet of residential refuse vehicles used with shared-can collection. The first monster vehicle was dubbed "Godzilla." A few years later Mike Wallace of "60 Minutes" visited the city for a special program on its innovative achievements.

Fashion Square was joined by Scottsdale's second major shopping center, Los Arcos Mall, which was built at the corner of Scottsdale and McDowell roads in 1969. One of the earliest shops on Fifth Avenue was the Scandinavian, where Christmas items from around the world were available year-round.

The arts were developing with even more fervor, and West Main Street became "gallery row." Along it was The Art Wagon, literally named because its partners, Suzanne Brown and Elaine Horwitch, first sold art from a station wagon in which they made house calls. The Scottsdale National Indian Arts Exhibition, organized in 1961 by Paul Huldermann and Lloyd Kiva New, attracted entrants from throughout the continental United States. The show grew in stature and popularity and was a launching pad for many of today's successful Indian artists, including Fritz Scholder, Charles Loloma, David Chethlahe Paladin, Grace Medicine Flower, Tony Begay, Kevin Redstar, and Joseph Lonewolf. Before the last show was held in 1976, the annual event was drawing a following similar to the Cowboy Artists of America exhibitions. Increasing costs and demands on an all-volunteer council finally ended the shows.

A special census in October 1965 put Scottsdale's population at 54,500, more than five times the figure of five years earlier. That made it the third largest city in the state after Phoenix and Tucson. The announcement capped a wave of civic rivalry with Mesa and Tempe, which were designated fourth and fifth largest, respectively. Scottsdale was now considered a "boom town," and its careful municipal planning soon would pay off.

Opposite page
The Center for the Arts is situated at the south end of the Civic Center complex area. Here cool ponds and striking sculptures accent a lush grassy walking mall. Top photo by Rick Mueller Photography

Above
Scottsdale's City Hall complex, designed by noted Southwestern architect Bennie Gonzales, includes a pond with sculptures and live mute swans. Photo by Bob Petley, Phoenix, Arizona

Right
Bruce Law carved this olivewood bust of Chaplain Scott from trees planted in 1895. The bust may be viewed in City Hall. Photo by Rick Mueller Photography

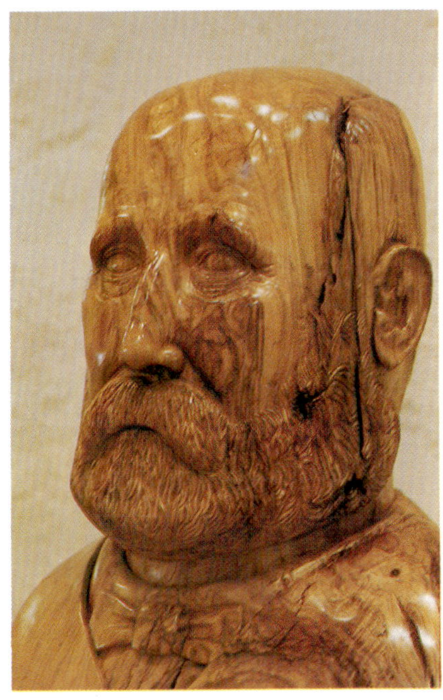

CHAPTER SIX

Coming of Age In A New Age

The expansion northward of the city was sparked by development of McCormick Ranch in the early 1970s. This view of The Inn at McCormick Ranch was photographed in 1977 before extensive residential and commercial building had begun. The view is to the northeast with Scottsdale Road across the center. Courtesy, Bill McLemore

By 1970 Scottsdale was no longer known only as "The West's Most Western Town." It also had established a new reputation; it was becoming known as a sophisticated suburban community with an exceptional cultural environment and fashion center. The town's early identity as a small, quiet, rural community had evolved into that of a haven for artists, artists supported by tourists.

The city's resort reputation attracted celebrity visitors—Mamie Eisenhower, Zsa Zsa Gabor, Mary Martin, Walter Cronkite, Tommy Smothers, John Wayne, Rick Nelson, Bob Newhart, Bob Hope, and Wayne Newton among them. They came to play golf, sit in the sun, ride horseback, and buy or sell horses—especially Arabians. Screen star Mary Pickford owned property at the northwest corner of Scottsdale and McDowell roads.

During three decades of intense growth, there had been major changes in the traditional Scottsdale scene. A fire on April 12, 1970, destroyed The Adobe House. The venerable building had served the community long and well as the Blount home and first school, a cheese factory, a guest ranch, a town library, and, finally, to house city arts and crafts classes. Its demise marked the end of one era and the beginning of another for Scottsdale.

Since its incorporation in 1951, the city had been developing as a long, narrow area with Scottsdale Road running straight down the center. The middle of town remained at Main and Scottsdale roads until the 1970s, when development moved north. It was the only possible growth direction because the Salt River Pima-Maricopa Indian Community was on the eastern border, Phoenix and the town of Paradise Valley on the western, and Tempe on the southern.

The 1970 census still put Scottsdale in place as the state's third largest city with a population of 67,823. In area it covered just over 68 square miles. Four years later annexations had expanded the population to 78,560 and the terrain to 89 square miles.

Now the city's master plan began to pay off in major residential developments. In 1970 Kaiser Aetna bought the Fowler McCormick Ranch property of 4,000-plus acres for $12.1 million. The firm hired 17 land-use experts and former city planner George Fretz to chart the development of this gigantic real-estate project with an eye to recreation design, marketing environment, and hydrology. The

Among the pieces of outdoor art that may be viewed in Scottsdale's Civic Center area are Louise Nevelson's Windows to the West *(left) and Bennie Gonzales'* The Children's Fountain *(below). Photos by Tom Johnson*

Taliesin West has been Frank Lloyd Wright's Southwestern headquarters since the late 1930s. Courtesy, Taliesin West

Chief Shatka Bear Step, who was raised by Indians, interpreted the Lord's Prayer in Indian sign language for many years as a part of the Parada del Sol. Courtesy, Bob Ross Photos

Gainey Ranch was the next to go on the market for housing. This led to the building of three major resorts on the ranch property—The Registry Resort, Scottsdale Conference Center, and The Inn at McCormick Ranch. Their luxurious accommodations were a far cry from the town's first tourist facility, the homey Underhill veranda-enhanced house at the northwest corner of Scottsdale and Indian School roads.

The city's first college, two-year Scottsdale Community College, opened in 1970 on leased Salt River Indian Community land to the east of the city. The architecture and programs of the college were influenced by the heritage of Pima and Maricopa Indians who lived nearby, some still in the small adobe-brick or rough daub-and-wattle houses of their early roots and others in modern homes. The campus has a horizontal appearance of low-profile buildings and broad, flat roofs with Indian designs integrated into the construction. The college spawned the Southwest Studies Institute, a program that focuses on the culture, geology, and history of Arizona and the Southwest, combining lectures with field trips. Enrollment was approximately 7,000 in the early 1980s.

In 1973 the city's social services center was established in the redeveloped Vista del Camino area, providing counseling, crisis intervention, economic assistance, a health clinic, housing, an emergency food bank, and other help projects. A downtown Senior Center offering recreational, educational, and human services to the elderly was also built.

Scottsdale continued to anchor its special identity as a winter outdoor-living city with unusual activities. Increasing numbers of people were coming to walk around in the sunshine and fresh air to browse in shops and galleries and to enjoy the grassy municipal mall with its unusual sculptures.

The Scottsdale Symphony Orchestra, begun with four strings and a French horn in 1974, developed into a 105-piece performing group directed by Irving Fleming. It played to standing-room-only audiences at the Scottsdale Center in November 1975.

In 1980 Molly the Trolley, a rubber-tired, red-and-yellow cable car replica, rolled onto the scene to become a peacemaker between the feuding Old Town and Fifth Avenue merchants. Both groups were vying for the tourist trade, and the trolleys were available throughout the entire year to transport an estimated quarter-million tourists and townies among the various shopping areas and resorts. No fares were charged; costs were subsidized by advertising on the vehicles. Residents and tourists alike were given a choice of transportation around shopping areas. They could travel in a horse-drawn carriage, automobile, stagecoach, a trolley, or on foot.

By the 1980s more than 200,000 spectators a year attended the Parada del Sol, which gained the distinction of being the nation's longest horse-drawn parade. The three-day rodeo, with its 350-some entrants, is listed in the top 100 attractions by American tour promoters. It also was cited by the Professional Rodeo Cowboy Association as among the top 10 professional events in North America. A special feature for many years was the interpretation of the "Lord's Prayer" in Indian sign language by Chief Shatka Bear Step, an Anglo jewelsmith who was raised by Indians.

Scottsdale also was attracting small businesses, clean industry, and office complexes. A fashion-oriented shopping mall had brought statewide attention in 1974 when the Texas-based Sakowitz firm established its first store in Arizona, the keystone for Camelview Plaza on Camelback Road west of Scottsdale Road. The Arizona Bank had one of the city's first commercial high-rise structures in the complex, and the plaza later was expanded by Bullock's of California. McCormick Ranch established other shopping areas, and contrasting hubs developed north of downtown: the Hilton Village area, The Borgata, Lincoln Plaza, and one at Scottsdale and Shea.

William Jenkins served as mayor from 1974 to 1980. A high school teacher, he continued the work of the citizens' STEP committees. He later served as president of the Scottsdale Historical Society. Courtesy, City of Scottsdale

Through the years the city's strong downtown high-rise ordinance permitted a maximum of 36-foot heights, allowing 60-foot-heights only in regional shopping centers. Several structures were built before the ordinance took effect, including the Scottsdale Towers Hotel and Arizona Bank. Instead, small, one-story office buildings, many with Spanish-style courtyards, filled the downtown area. Several nationally known firms chose Scottsdale for their new headquarters, among them Armour Research Center, Sentry Insurance, W.A. Krueger Company, Corporate Jets, and Pharmaceutical Card Systems.

Despite large corporate and chain hotel operations coming into town, the personal touch still survived in many places. In 1976 Joe Miller and his wife Evie, the bartender and waitress at El Chorro Lodge, took over El Chorro after Mark Gruber's death.

The means of recording the city's colorful life-style were expanded beyond the daily newspaper in 1976 by the *Scottsdale Quarterly,* a people-oriented magazine run by a husband-and-wife team, publisher Bob Rinehart and editor Marge Rinehart. The 18-year residents had published the monthly *Carefree Enterprise* since 1963. A second magazine began as *The Rancher,* a newsletter for residents of McCormick Ranch. It was purchased in 1981 by former Wisconsin weekly editor-publisher Hoyt Johnson (who was assisted by his wife and sons), who later started the monthly *Scottsdale Scene* magazine. Cable television expanded the community's media operations in the 1980s as Scottsdale United

Right
This bright crimson cowboy hat represents Scottsdale's international reputation as having a blend of the rugged Old West with horseback riding, rodeos, cookouts, and trail rides, and the sophisticated New West of art galleries, concerts, and luxurious resorts. Courtesy, Scottsdale Chamber of Commerce

A winter-season intertown rubber-wheeled trolley system takes residents and tourists around to shopping centers and resorts. Here it rolls along Brown Avenue, the old mission church in the background. Courtesy, Scottsdale Chamber of Commerce

Every spring an arts festival is held at the Scottsdale Center for the Arts. Pictured here is the 1980 festival.

The 1973 Parada del Sol traveled down Scottsdale Road in front of the Wigwam Department Store. Photo by Bob Petley

Herb Drinkwater served as a city councilman before being elected as mayor in 1980 and reelected in 1984. He came to central Arizona with his family as a child and has lived most of his life in Scottsdale. He has been kidded about his resemblance to Chaplain Winfield Scott, both having bald heads, beards, and mustaches. Some who have seen the olivewood bust of the town's founder in City Hall (see page 83) have thought it was the modern-day mayor. Courtesy, City of Scottsdale

Cable refurbished the empty Loloma Elementary School for its headquarters. The Scottsdale Historical Society also located its office and mini-museum there.

The city's charter government remained stable, operating with a city council, city manager, mayor, and six councilmen elected at large for four-year terms. Councilman William Jenkins was appointed mayor in 1974 to fill the unexpired term of Bud Tims, who was elected to the Arizona Corporation Commission. Jenkins, a high school teacher, was reelected to serve until 1980. One part of the municipal plan was to have public works employees trained as fire "wranglers" to assist the regular force. And the STEP committees continued providing input to city officials.

The long-talked-about Indian Bend Wash flood control and greenbelt project was started in the spring of 1973, after nearly $4 million in damage from errant waters the previous year. The project was a six-phase $4 million plan that had the Army Corps of Engineers handling half the cost, the city offering flood-control bond financing of nearly one million dollars, and the remainder coming from other city and county funds. The final phase of the greenbelt project was begun late in 1982 as runoff channels and pipelines were constructed along the Arizona Canal from the Indian Bend Wash west to 68th Street.

The focal point of the greenbelt, Indian School Park, which was completed on January 19, 1980, at a cost of $3.8 million, covered 60 acres and was paid for by local bed-tax funds from the tourist industry. It contains the project's visitors' center. One of four parks within walking distance of residential areas, it has 13 lighted tennis courts, four baseball fields, four racquetball courts, two basketball courts, 12 lighted shuffleboard courts, and courts for horseshoes, volleyball, croquet, and bocci ball. There also are picnic areas, bike trails, a model-boating lake, and a children's play area.

By 1970 Scottsdale had built another 10 schools. Enrollment was 28,632 in 1972, and by the nation's bicentennial year of 1976 there were two more elementary units, Chaparral High School, and a vocational-technical center. By the early 1980s, with 14 elementary and four high schools, the scramble to provide enough space stopped. Population trends had begun to reverse, resulting in declining enrollment. In 1983 there were 18,563 students, and the total is expected to stabilize at 15,000 by the late 1980s.

Scottsdale Community Hospital, a 340-bed osteopathic facility that opened in 1970, was expanded in 1983 with an 80-bed long-term care unit and again the following year with a second story and another 100 beds. Scottsdale Memorial Hospital expanded on its original site in the 1970s, building five outlying health facilities. In 1984 Scottsdale Memorial Hospital North, a 120-bed facility that includes a critical care unit, opened in northern Scottsdale. A psychiatric facility, Scottsdale Camelback Hospital, opened in the mid-town area in the late 1970s.

Three locally owned banks soon opened—the Bank of Scottsdale in the 1970s and Scottsdale Commercial Bank and National Bank of Scottsdale in the 1980s.

In the mid-1970s Scottsdale had a population of 80,000, compared to 2,032 when it was incorporated only 15 years earlier. There were 31,200 households with 56 percent of the population earning between $10,000 and $25,000 a year and 50 percent of the homes valued at between $25,000 and $50,000. Seventy-eight percent of the residents owned their own homes. There was five percent unemployment, and 32 percent of households included working women.

Some of the olive trees Chaplain Scott planted in 1895 still provide shade. Photo by Tom Johnson

Councilman Herb Drinkwater resigned in 1978 after eight years on the council and in 1980 won a four-year mayoral term, and was reelected in 1984. His campaigns focused on a theme that had predominated in elections since Malcolm White became the first mayor—to retain the small-town atmosphere while keeping pace with the needs of a larger community. "We have a neat city," says Drinkwater. "It has grown from a small town to one of the finest cities in the country. I want to help keep the way of life here the way it is." That, however, was proving to be a difficult task.

By 1983 the former barren desert of northern Scottsdale was the hub of an expensive building boom, residences going for a median price of $119,000 as compared to $67,000 in other parts of metropolitan Phoenix. The high price tags were due to Scottsdale's many townhouses, condos, and single-family homes, some situated on man-made lakes stocked with fish and available for water sports. One subdivision was built around an 18-hole golf course designed by Jack Nicklaus. Nearby another posh hotel opened in 1984, Loew's Paradise Valley Resort, so-named because it was situated on an island within the city of Scottsdale. Its architecture reflected the Southwestern-Indian influence epitomized by Frank Lloyd Wright's block design at the Arizona Biltmore.

Scottsdale moved into its greatest period of growth in the mid-1980s. It was the site of 50 percent of Arizona's resorts, with 38 resorts, hotels, and motels offering 5,770 rooms and meeting facilities; several award-winning restaurants among 200 locations; some 90 art galleries; and about 2,500 retail stores. Seasonal events in addition to the Parada del Sol and major league baseball training that drew visitors included festivals focusing on the culinary arts, arts and crafts, Shakespearean programs, jazz and chamber music concert series, Arabian horses, classic cars, golf tournaments, and even psychic fairs.

The Borgata is a posh shopping plaza designed as the recreation of an Italian Renaissance-era village. It features exclusive shops, galleries, and restaurants connected by cobblestone walkways. Courtesy, Scottsdale Chamber of Commerce

Scottsdale High School opened in 1923 and that spring the graduating class consisted of three students. Pictured here is the school's "300 Building," also known as Old Main. In the spring of 1983 the school closed. Courtesy, William Jenkins

Every year John Gardiner's Tennis Ranch, on the north slope of Camelback Mountain, is the location of celebrity tournaments for charity, attracting politicians, entertainment stars, and fans. Courtesy, John Gardiner's Tennis Ranch

The Phoenician Resort Community links its ultramodern life-style to the roots of Jokake Inn, built in the 1930s as Scottsdale's first resort facility. The twin mission-style adobe towers overlook the new development as silent sentinels that recall the past. Courtesy, Stricklan Communications

May Vanderhoof Mathis, born in May 1900, was the first Anglo child born in Scottsdale. Having lived all her life in the community, she has seen it evolve from a dusty rural crossroads village to a world-renowned tourist center. Courtesy, Scottsdale Daily Progress

By 1983 there were six major industrial/business parks and more than 40 retail shopping centers. When the chamber of commerce surveyed major employers to find out why they had located their businesses in Scottsdale, the responses focused on the area's living and working life-styles, its growth and profit potential, the city government, and, of course, the climate. (The National Weather Service affirmed that Scottsdale has sunny days an average 86 percent of the year, with about seven inches of rain annually, making it an ideal location for tennis, golf, horseback riding, and other outdoor activities.) Employers cited other advantages of Scottsdale as well, including reasonably priced land, pro-business state and local governments, a high-quality work force (better-educated, innovative and creative, living an active life-style), lower tax structure, skilled labor pool, fine parks, excellent schools and medical facilities, a variety of housing, and favorable utility rates.

The Scottsdale of the 1980s had 103,000 people in 46,600 households. The median age of residents was 36. The largest portion of the population, 25 percent, had an income of between $35,000 and $50,000, with 16 percent above $25,000, and 15 percent above $50,000. In terms of race, 93 percent were white, three percent Mexican-American, one percent black, and three percent of other ethnic backgrounds. With continuing annexation to the north, including a 25 percent increase of 36 square miles in mid-1984, Scottsdale covered 181 square miles.

The new Scottsdale differed in many ways from the small Western town of the early 1960s. As recalled by *Scottsdale Daily Progress* publisher Jonathan Marshall:

It was a town that was relaxed, with a lot of enthusiasm among its residents, where people were excited by what was happening. There was excitement about creativity in schools, and people were willing to experiment.

Most of the streets were not paved, and that was sort of quaint and nice. You still saw horses downtown; people would ride to Lute's and Earl's, and the Indians would come into town and sit on benches in front of the market. There was a feeling of a Western town. It was a friendly place, and personalized; you'd go in a restaurant and always see someone you knew, and you'd never stand in line for a movie.

Chaplain Scott never would have recognized his homestead neighborhood. Two Scottsdale Financial Center buildings, built by Western Devcor and valued at $90 million, were constructed at Indian School and Scottsdale roads near the site of the former Graves Guest Ranch and what used to be the chaplain's backyard. The firm paid $29.67 a square foot for the land as compared to

Scott's cost of two and one-half dollars an acre in 1888. To the east, One Civic Center Plaza, a $11.5 million, three-story office complex, took over the corner of Indian School Road and Civic Center Plaza, not far from the former home of artist Marjorie Thomas.

No, despite his foresight, Chaplain Scott never could have pictured modern-day Scottsdale with its year-round population of some 100,000 boosted every winter by thousands of visitors from across the nation and around the world. Nor could he have imagined the 20th-century town with its spacious downtown walking mall accented by restaurants, shops, and glinting sculptures; a tourist center of worldwide fame because of its luxurious resorts, enticing boutiques, swank shopping centers, elegant restaurants, and celebrated art galleries; or a city with a busy winter season of concerts and exhibits plus outdoor activities of golf, tennis, and horseback riding. No, the chaplain could not possibly have foreseen his small dream community stretching far from its simple rural roots to emerge as a city with an international reputation as an oasis for leisure and the arts, a blend of the rugged Old West and the sophisticated New West.

Above
Marjorie Thomas came to Scottsdale with her mother and brother in 1909 just after graduation from the School of the Museum of Fine Arts in Boston. The family first rented a cottage until the government opened up land in the desert for homesteading. She lived in Scottsdale until 1950, when she returned to the East for several years. Her artwork was featured in one-woman shows in Phoenix and the East. Courtesy, Thelma Steiner Holveck/Labeula Steiner Mowry

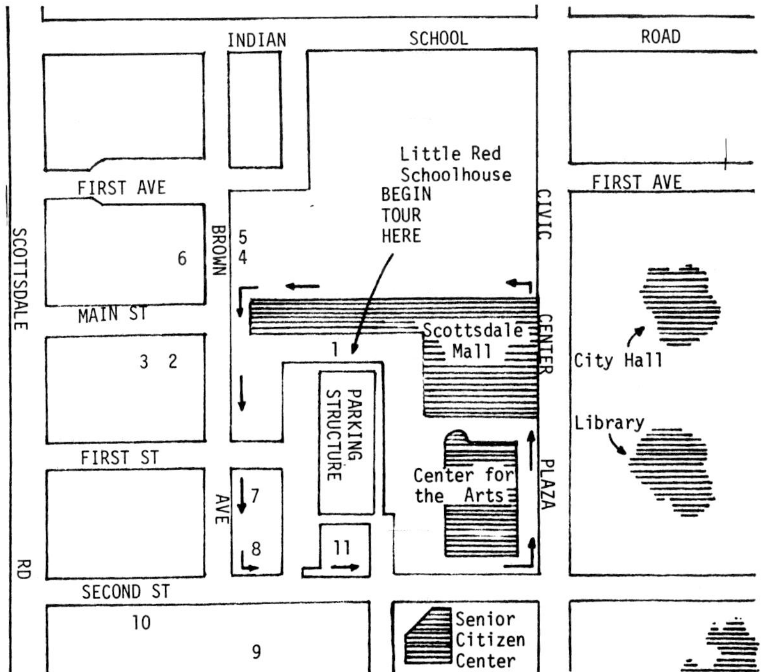

Left
A self-guided walking tour of historical Old-Town Scottsdale takes 45 minutes and covers 12 locations, starting at the Little Red Schoolhouse, 1; 2. site of first general store and post office; 3. town's first bank; 4. Johnny Rose's Pool Hall; 5. adobe building began as general store; 6. first post office building; 7. Catholic church; 8. blacksmith shop; 9. cotton gin; 10. olive trees; 11. Los Olivos Restaurant; 12. Scottsdale Center for the Arts, on the site of the adobe pit used to make bricks for many early buildings. Courtesy, Scottsdale Historical Society

CHAPTER SEVEN

Partners in Progress

Some of the children in this 1912 photo grew up to become leaders in the Scottsdale business community. Pictured here are: (at left, on horseback) Alvin Brown and Helen Hayden; (front row, standing) Edward "Buster" Graves, Mary Graves, Nina Bassham, Frank Coldwell, George "Bud" Serviss, James Vanderhoof, Lenore Coldwell, Adeline Coldwell, Carl Bassham, Nora Holmes, John Elmer Williams, Polly Elliott, William Miller, Tom Coldwell, Laura Elliott; (second row, left) Mrs. Frank Last (teacher), George Thomas (in hat), unknown, Ellsworth Brown, Myrtle Elliott, Stanley Ellis Thomas, May Vanderhoof (rein in hand); (third row) Grace Thomas, Ruth Brown, Mrs. Walter P. Smith (in hat). The red brick schoolhouse, which was erected in 1909, houses the Scottsdale Chamber of Commerce. Courtesy, City of Scottsdale

The land that now is Scottsdale was known in the 1880s as a paradise for rattlesnakes, gila monsters, and its first settlers, the Indians, before Chaplain Winfield Scott visited the Valley of the Salt River and became a one-man chamber of commerce touting the area as rich, fertile, and full of promise.

With an elevation of 1,290 feet, soft water, spectacular mountain ranges, and fertile soil, Chaplain Scott's settlement 12 miles east of Phoenix became a desirable place to both visit and live for those suffering from upper respiratory ailments. With a crop of barley; citrus orchards; grape vineyards; and apricot, peach, almond, and nectarine trees, the farming and resort community had been launched in 1889.

Today the farming community, open space, and dry desert climate have been replaced by a thriving metropolis of 103,000 people who came to Scottsdale to enjoy an attractive life-style and a pleasant working environment.

Scottsdale's orderly development just didn't happen; it was planned from the beginning by the city council and the business sector working closely together to ensure a community free of many big-city faults. There is an absence of glaring neon lights, high-rise structures (with the exception of the Arizona Bank Building), and outdoor display signs.

And there still is a feeling of open space as one traverses the length and breadth of Scottsdale, viewing Camelback Mountain, Mummy Mountain, and the McDowells, the acres of greenbelts, lakes, and other amenities that keep the "snowbirds" returning year after year and the residents delighted they were fortunate enough to be transplanted in Scottsdale, "The West's Most Western Town."

The organizations whose stories are detailed on the following pages have chosen to support this important literary and civic project. They illustrate the variety of ways in which individuals and their businesses have contributed to the growth and development of Scottsdale. The civic involvement of the city's businesses, learning institutions, and local government, in partnership with its citizens, has made Scottsdale a first-class place to live and work.

SCOTTSDALE HISTORICAL SOCIETY

The need for a historical society in Scottsdale became evident to long-time residents more than 15 years ago when one of the town's last historical landmarks, the Little Red Schoolhouse, faced demolition.

In order to save the one-room schoolhouse from destruction, citizens rallied in support of a Scottsdale Historical Society in June 1968. At that time city councilman Bill Jenkins, later to become mayor and more recently president of the Society, and Paul Huldermann, chairman of the city's fine arts commission, called a meeting "to start preserving items of historical interest to our city."

"Hopefully, once a historical society is organized, the interest in and support of such an organization will be self generating," Jenkins said at the time. The first objective of the group was to locate people who played an important role in the early life of the community and to receive artifacts and memorabilia from early-day families for the future Scottsdale Museum.

Fourteen people attended the first organizational meeting on July 11, 1968, held in the City Hall Conference Room. Former Mayor Mort Kimsey and Leldon Windes, who taught in the Scottsdale School District for 30 years, were chosen co-chairmen while Stan Crews was named secretary. The founding event was well-covered by the local newspaper as well as by two television stations.

Coinciding with the establishment of the Society was the launching of the "Save the Little Red Schoolhouse" drive. By the new organization's second meeting, on July 25, 1968, some 500 signatures had been obtained to save the school; a number of photographs and documents had been offered to the Society by residents; and two art teachers, Betty Crews and Jeannette Yount, offered to arrange the first historical display for the city's dedication of the newly completed Civic Center building in October 1968.

Over the years the Society has gained recognition for supporting the preservation of numerous historical landmarks, including the successful preservation of the Little Red Schoolhouse which became an Arizona Historic Property in 1973. The group has for several years sponsored a walking tour of Old Town Scottsdale initiated by Dick Lynch, who served five years as president of the organization and helped raise its membership from 35 to more than 100. Under Lynch's leadership the Society also compiled a large research file of tapes and oral history interviews and instituted Preservation Week activities for Scottsdale.

In June 1981 a Scottsdale Museum Fund was established with $1,000 seed money from the Society. The fund has reached $12,000, with the dream of a museum very much alive today.

Memorabilia of early-day Scottsdale currently has a home in the organization's new office and mini-museum, located in the United Cable Television of Scottsdale corporate headquarters at 3720 North Marshall Way. Formerly the Loloma School, the 1928 landmark is now a City of Scottsdale Historic Property. United Cable restored the property and dedicated a room to the Society in 1983. Board meetings are held there twice a month and historical displays may be viewed weekdays from noon to 3 p.m., from October to June. Scottsdale Historical Society meetings, which are open to the public free of charge and feature entertaining programs by prominent historians and storytellers, are held the first Thursday of each month from October to June.

George Thomas (right), the first Anglo male child born in Scottsdale, examines the school bell that called him to classes in the Little Red Schoolhouse starting back in 1909. With him is the Reverend Eugene Maguire, pastor of Our Lady of Perpetual Help Catholic Church, where the bell had been put in the tower. It was placed on display in the converted schoolhouse, housing the Chamber of Commerce, and now is in the museum of the Scottsdale Historical Society.

DALE ANDERSON'S RESTAURANTS

It was quite by accident that Scottsdale restaurateur Dale Anderson ended up in the restaurant business, but it is no accident that he has become one of the most prominent businessmen in the city, entertaining everyone from royalty to local clientele in his several dining establishments.

When Anderson left St. James, Minnesota, in 1947, he knew only that he did not want to follow in his father's footsteps in the lumber business. He attended Gustavas Adolphus College for two years, then joined the Marines. After completing his military service, Anderson came to the Valley of the Sun to work in the produce business for a man he met while in the Marines.

His 30-year restaurant career began with Lulu Belle's in 1954, when everyone in town acted like "wild and reckless cowboys." His job, first as assistant manager and later as manager, included everything from taking guns away from the town drunks when they became unruly to breaking up fights.

Anderson stayed at Lulu Belle's until he opened Dale Anderson's Restaurant at First Avenue and Marshall Way in 1963. From the Marshall Way operation, he now operates six restaurants: three in Scottsdale and one each in Tempe, Mesa, and Tucson.

The first Dale Anderson's on Marshall Way had been a private residence with several individual rooms, inspiring him to develop a concept that features fine dining in a cozy, homelike atmosphere.

The Other Place, located at 7101 East Lincoln Drive, is one of four restaurants with that name in the state. It features a Spanish motif.

He operated that first Dale Anderson's for six years before opening The Other Place, at 7101 East Lincoln Drive. Arriving at the Other Place name, which has become famous throughout the state, was somewhat unconventional. In 1969, after purchasing the restaurant, which was located in the main lodge of an old Scottsdale resort—the Diamond Lazy K—and while overseeing its renovation, Anderson kept saying to his staff, "I'm going to the other place." The name stuck, and since that time a second Other Place opened in June 1975 in Tempe's Fiesta Inn; a third opened in 1979 at the Dobson Inn in Mesa; and a fourth began operation in 1982 at The Inn at the Airport in Tucson.

Yet another Anderson restaurant, The Quilted Bear, at 6316 North Scottsdale Road, a few blocks east of the Lincoln Drive Other Place, is one of the most popular Scottsdale dining establishments. Carrying out a bear theme, there are bears of various sizes and shapes and colorful patchwork materials accenting the furnishings. Also featured is a huge stained-glass window depicting a bear.

The sixth restaurant, a long overdue Dale Anderson's specializing in seafood, opened in October 1984 in the new Scottsdale Centre at 7373 Scottsdale Road North.

During the past 30 years, Dale Anderson has devoted untold hours to the development of Scottsdale. He served as president of the Scottsdale Chamber of Commerce and twice served on its board of directors, and was president of the Scottsdale Charros, the Scottsdale Rotary Club, and the Arizona Restaurant Association. He is a founder and director of the Bank of Scottsdale. During Scottsdale's peak growth years, Anderson was involved in many areas of planning and development of the city of Scottsdale and served on many committees.

The Quilted Bear restaurant, located at 6316 North Scottsdale Drive, carries out a bear theme and features a huge stained-glass window depicting a bear.

SCOTTSDALE BOARD OF REALTORS, INC.

One of mankind's oldest businesses, the transfer of real property, has prospered in Scottsdale over the past 20 years with much credit for that prosperity directed at the Scottsdale Board of REALTORS, Inc.

The board has fostered a long history of service to the community not only through efforts to give the buying and selling public competent, ethical handling of transactions, but also through a variety of projects that have helped promote Scottsdale.

The Scottsdale association, with a current membership of 2,386, established itself on November 13, 1963, as the Scottsdale Real Estate Board, Inc., with 20 members. The name was subsequently changed on May 4, 1973, to the Scottsdale Board of REALTORS, Inc.

The group presently is the largest organization in Scottsdale. Its purpose is to unite the real estate industry for the purpose of effectively exerting a combined influence upon matters affecting real estate interests, to promote and maintain the high standards of conduct in the transaction of real estate business expressed in the National Association of REALTORS Code of Ethics, and to advance the civic development and economic growth of Scottsdale.

Breaking records in real estate transactions over the past 20 years has been the rule rather than the exception for Scottsdale real estate agents and brokers. In 1965 the Scottsdale Multiple Listing Service, which is the prime service of the association, had 19 brokers for a total of 288 salespeople. Five years later, in 1973, there were 99 member firms and 939 associates.

Another milestone was heralded on November 23, 1966, when sales in Scottsdale exceeded one million dollars for any one-week period since the board's founding. When the service first started, sales totaled about $.25 million a week. Four years later, in 1970, an estimated $80 million in real estate transactions had taken place with medium-price homes selling for $15,000 to $28,000. At that time the board had 83 members, 675 salesmen, and was the fourth-largest board in the state. In 1971 the dollar volume jumped over $119 million, and in 1972 the figure surpassed $136 million. By comparison, during one week in October 1983, the listing service had 136 sales for a total dollar volume of $18,679,800 with the average home costing $137,000.

In 1969 the board moved into its own headquarters at 4221 North Scottsdale Road, after making its home in a rented suite at 719 Old Scottsdale Road for two years. Since then the organization has progressed from a part-time secretarial service to a full-time executive vice-president with a staff of eight housed in the two-story Spanish-style office complex.

Henry Gruenemeier, the board's executive vice-president, has served in that capacity since 1972, watching the city grow from a population of 7,200 when he arrived in Scottsdale 26 years ago to a population of more than 100,000 today. "I feel as a realtor we physically sell this city every day, every acre, every lot, house by house, and business by business," he says. "We make our living by selling every block of it. It's an amazing place to live and to have children."

The officers and directors of the 1984 board are dedicated to helping the city grow.

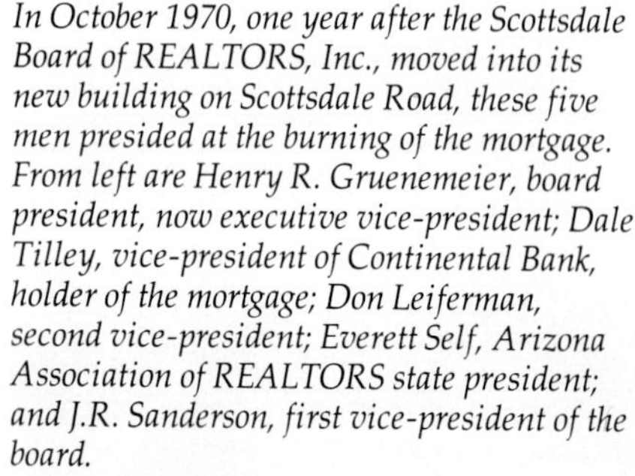

In October 1970, one year after the Scottsdale Board of REALTORS, Inc., moved into its new building on Scottsdale Road, these five men presided at the burning of the mortgage. From left are Henry R. Gruenemeier, board president, now executive vice-president; Dale Tilley, vice-president of Continental Bank, holder of the mortgage; Don Leiferman, second vice-president; Everett Self, Arizona Association of REALTORS state president; and J.R. Sanderson, first vice-president of the board.

MESSINGER MORTUARY & CHAPEL, INC.

In the days before Scottsdale developed into a world-renowned resort city, Arizona State Representative Paul R. Messinger went about his daily tasks of milking the cows at the family's grade A dairy located on 10 acres of land at the southeast corner of Miller and Indian School roads where the city's first mortuary, Messinger Mortuary & Chapel, now stands.

When the mortuary opened its doors on May 10, 1959, Indian School Road was still a two-lane paved country road bounded on the south by a major irrigation ditch and on the north by a wastewater ditch lined with pomegranate trees. Miller Road had just been paved and the new mortuary was still surrounded by a dairy farm, an alfalfa field, and new building projects of Our Lady of Perpetual Help Church. The Messinger family had sold the 10-acre parcel in 1955 to the Catholic diocese.

The summer before the mortuary was built, when Scottsdale was less than one square mile in size, the Messinger family asked the city to annex their 10 acres at Miller and Indian School roads so that the proposed mortuary could be inspected by the town's only building inspector, Walter Donn, because Maricopa County did no inspections. The city fathers agreed to rezone the property only if the family agreed to provide Scottsdale with 24-hour-a-day, seven-day-a-week ambulance service, which they did until 1968. At one time, the Messingers operated five ambulances, with the service being the first commercially operated service in the city.

Messinger Mortuary & Chapel, Inc., 7601 East Indian School Road, is a family business founded by the Messinger family: Paul R. Messinger, funeral director and embalmer; his wife, Cora R., corporate secretary and in charge of general office operation; William H. Messinger, treasurer; his wife, Vera F. Messinger, who died in 1980; and Paul's brother, Philip W. Messinger, vice-president. However, Paul and Cora Messinger, and their son Kendrick, a licensed funeral director and embalmer, are actively involved in the business today.

During the first year of operation the Messingers had only two employees, Ray Morehead and Jerry Bullock. They served 75 families that first year and today, nearly a quarter-century later, there are 20 employees and over 10,000 families have been served.

The Messingers joined with four other funeral directors and two individuals to start Paradise Memorial Gardens, 9300 East Shea Boulevard, in 1968. The city granted zoning, but the state denied a state license. Court action followed with the Arizona Supreme Court ruling in favor of the applicants, thus paving the way for the cemetery and the first interment in February 1974. In 1983 the Messingers became the sole owners of Paradise Memorial Gardens, a 40-acre cemetery.

Paul R. Messinger, director of Messinger Mortuary & Chapel, Inc., has also represented District 28 in the Arizona State House of Representatives since1979. Portrait by Gittings.

The Messinger Mortuary & Chapel is located at 7601 East Indian School Road, Scottsdale.

In the Arizona State House of Representatives, Paul Messinger has represented District 28 since 1979. He served on the Scottsdale City Council from 1971 to 1976 and as vice-mayor from 1974 to 1975. He was chairman of the citizens committee that brought the Scottsdale Community College to Scottsdale, served on the Scottsdale Airport Advisory Commission, and has been president and national officer of several professional funeral associations. He was twice appointed to the State Board of Funeral Directors and served as the board's president for two terms.

SENTRY INSURANCE

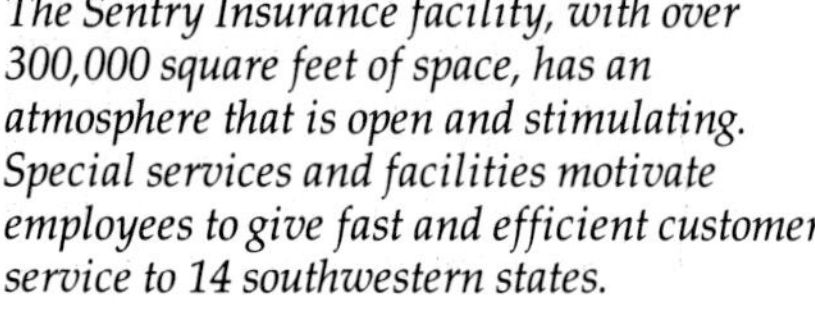

The Sentry Insurance facility, with over 300,000 square feet of space, has an atmosphere that is open and stimulating. Special services and facilities motivate employees to give fast and efficient customer service to 14 southwestern states.

The people who organized Sentry Insurance, then called Hardware Mutual, in 1904 in Wisconsin probably never realized it would one day grow into a diversifed international group of more than 90 companies with assets in excess of $2.2 billion.

Today the Sentry family not only includes insurance companies but other businesses such as radio and cable television, manufacturing, oil and gas exploration, financial services, automobile leasing, and a management firm specializing in affirmative action.

Sentry employs nearly 10,000 people in 57 cities throughout the United States and in seven foreign countries. Nearly one-quarter of the employees work in Stevens Point, Wisconsin, which is the corporate headquarters. There are four major centers, of which Scottsdale is one.

After many years of rapid growth, Sentry centralized its operations to become more flexible to changing consumer needs. It was during this time, in 1976, that the Sentry Center West Home Office was established in Scottsdale in what was the newly developing 4,200-acre McCormick Ranch, a planned community of commercial and residential living. Sentry was the first commercial business to be developed on 103 acres in the prestigious McCormick Ranch Center, a multimillion-dollar commercial, financial, retail, and light industrial complex.

The state-of-the-art Scottsdale Center West, with 300,000 square feet, is designed in an integrated campus style of Neo-Hispanic-Calaboose architecture to maintain the southwestern atmosphere. Within the complex is an educational training area consisting of four fully equipped classrooms, a cafeteria seating 400 people, and a seminar room for 300 people, along with a medical suite, large mail room, and legal library. Then, in a separate conference and amenities center, there are 19 rooms and two suites for overnight visitors and employees enrolled in training courses, as well as physical fitness facilities available to employees during and after work. These amenities include an exercise room, lighted tennis and inside racquetball courts, athletic field, and a swimming pool heated by solar energy.

When Sentry West opened its Scottsdale operation in 1976, the newly desert-landscaped regional office was surrounded by virgin desert. Today it is surrounded by luxury homes to the east and the new Scottsdale Memorial Hospital to the west.

Among the companies operating from the Scottsdale offices are The Sentry Insurance-A Mutual Company, the first venture to introduce the Plain Talk insurance policies, which cover cars, property, recreational vehicles, businesses, and personal and professional liability; Sentry Life Insurance Company, which offers life, health, disability, investment, and retirement plans for individuals and groups; Dairyland Insurance, which handles non-standard auto and motorcycle insurance; Great Southwest Fire Insurance Company, which underwrites unique fire and casualty risks; and Sentry Indemnity Company, which offers fire and casualty insurance through independent agents.

Sentry also prides itself on community involvement and being a good neighbor. Corporate official John Schwantes currently is president of the Scottsdale Chamber of Commerce, while other officers serve on the Scottsdale Planning Commission and the Human Services Commission.

At their annual meeting in 1903, members of the Wisconsin Retail Hardware Association organized their own insurance company.

MOTOROLA INC.

Motorola Inc., is one of the world's leading manufacturers of electronic equipment, systems, and components, with about 80,000 employees in major facilities in 15 countries and Puerto Rico and sales offices in more than 110 countries. The firm began its Valley of the Sun expansion project 35 years ago when a team of five engineers and technicians rented 6,000 square feet of office space in downtown Phoenix.

Today, from that small staff headed by the late Dr. Daniel E. Noble, former vice-president in charge of communications and electronics and director of research, Motorola has grown to more than 20,000 employees in the greater Phoenix area with approximately 6,000 based at the Scottsdale headquarters of the Government Electronics Group, located on 160 acres at 8201 East McDowell Road.

The GEG, formerly the Military Electronics Division, produces highly complex communications, radar, and tactical electronic equipment for defense and space applications. The equipment produced in Scottsdale is employed on most major U.S. manned and unmanned space flights, and the group's equipment and systems are widely used by the U.S. Department of Defense and throughout the Free World.

The parent company, founded in 1928 by Paul V. Galvin as the Galvin Manufacturing Corporation in Chicago, first produced a "battery eliminator" which allowed consumers to operate radios directly from household current instead of batteries. By 1937 Galvin had expanded into the radio business, making Motorola a household name. In the early 1940s the firm designed and developed the original "Walkie-Talkie" FM radio used during World War II. Perhaps the most significant discovery was the invention of the power transistor, which signaled the rise of Motorola as a significant manufacturer of transistors.

Dr. Daniel E. Noble, Motorola vice-chairman of the board, before the recently completed Motorola Research Center on 56th Street around 1951. All three Phoenix-based Motorola divisions were spawned in this building, constructed in 1950.

The original Government Electronics Group was located on 56th Street between Thomas and Indian School roads, where a 40,000-square-foot facility was constructed in and occupied by 1950. Rapid growth of the government division made it necessary to relocate by 1956, this time to a new 190,000-square-foot plant at McDowell and Hayden roads. The Hayden Plant, as it became known, grew by 1965 to over 350,000 square feet; by 1970 to over 700,000 square feet; and in 1984, with the completion of the Tactical Electronics Roosevelt Street Operation complex, the group's facilities in Scottsdale and Tempe totaled 1.6 million square feet.

The Government Electronics Group is divided into three business entities: the Communications Division, which also has a communications research facility in Gilbert; the Radar Operations, in Tempe; and Tactical Electronics Operations. James R. Lincicome, a corporate vice-president of Motorola Inc., is general manager of the Government Electronics Group, which also has sales offices in England, Italy, Japan, Malaysia, the Netherlands, Switzerland, and the Federal Republic of Germany.

In 1965 the City of Phoenix honored Motorola founder Paul Galvin by renaming a major thoroughfare the Galvin Parkway for his leadership in developing and expanding electronics in the Salt River Valley. Galvin's teammate, Dr. Noble, who died in 1980, planted the initial seeds in the Valley and nurtured their growth for more than 30 years. He became known as the Father of Arizona Industry for his industrial leadership and many contributions to technical education. As a tribute, the science library at Arizona State University is named the Daniel E. Noble Memorial Library.

Motorola's Government Electronics Group began in Scottsdale in 1956 as a 190,000-square-foot building at McDowell and Hayden roads. The group had expanded to a total of 1.6 million square feet by 1984. The facility is shown here in various stages of construction.

THE IMPECCABLE PIG

Quilts, baskets, copper, antique furniture, and food all go together at Scottsdale's The Impeccable Pig, where the dining experience is complemented by American primitives and French and English 18th- and 19th-century furnishings.

Nowhere else can one order shrimp scampi, a European salad plate, albacore tuna salad, or crab salad served with piping hot homemade rolls—and also buy the antique oak table and chairs where one is seated.

Owner of The Impeccable Pig, Dee Ann Skipton, has grown up with antiques all her life and was a collector before opening the combination antique-gourmet dining establishment in December 1979.

Her vocation as a nurse did not prepare her for the business world, but without hesitation she leased the building located at 7042 East Indian School Road and began a total renovation of 3,500 square feet which was expanded one year later to over 5,000 square feet.

The restaurant was an outgrowth of a gourmet cooking school that was operated by Ms. Skipton and her staff for about six months. People who came into the antique store began asking if they could purchase a sandwich, and soon the cooking school became a full-fledged restaurant with the dining area expanding to the elevated stage that had been built specifically for the cooking school.

Everything is prepared in a kitchen completely open to view by the public and equipped with one six-burner range-top stove and oven; there is no grill, no microwave, and no broiler. A French chef and assistant are allowed full reign to create menus and to name dishes.

"The only requirement is it must be good," Ms. Skipton says. "I truly feel that the public becomes my guest when they enter The Impeccable Pig. I want them to enjoy their experience here and look forward to returning." The Pig's recipes are in great demand and soon will be published in a new cookbook, *"Impeccable Tastes,"* by Ms. Skipton.

In the antique section, Ms. Skipton's Americana collection of old quilts are her favorite because they bring back fond memories. They are all handmade in the Midwest, as are other crafts such as hooked rugs, woven placemats, quilted animals, dolls, and jackets and vests. She purchases quality hand-crafted and folk-art recreations from craftsmen throughout the United States.

Dee Ann Skipton was reared in St. Joseph, Missouri, where her parents, Dr. and Mrs. Manning Grimes, still live and search for antiques to fill The Impeccable Pig's rooms. One item that remains a significant part of the antique store is the hand-carved Dentzel carousel pig that played a part in the naming of the establishment. "I wanted the logo to be an unusual animal, something people would remember," she said. "I wanted pigs to look impeccable."

Skipton first came to Scottsdale in 1944 as a visitor after her grandparents settled here. In 1968 she moved here permanently and has contributed to the community through her interest in the Marshall Way Association and the Scottsdale Chamber of Commerce. She also assists local charities.

Dee Ann Skipton, owner of The Impeccable Pig, is shown surrounded by early Americana treasures including a carousel horse brought from her parents' home in St. Joseph, Missouri. Photo courtesy of John Hall.

SCOTTSDALE MEMORIAL HOSPITAL

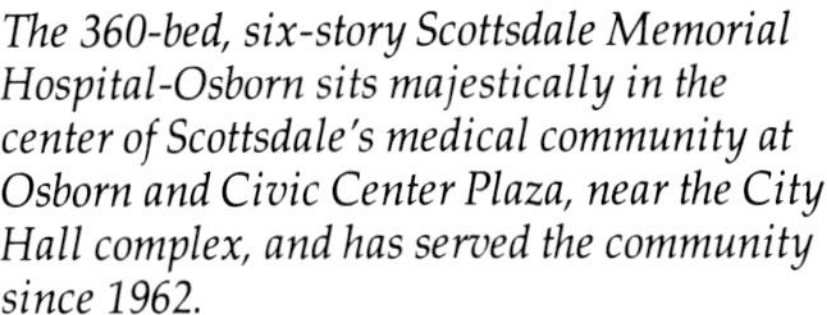

The 360-bed, six-story Scottsdale Memorial Hospital-Osborn sits majestically in the center of Scottsdale's medical community at Osborn and Civic Center Plaza, near the City Hall complex, and has served the community since 1962.

An attitude of caring has been nurtured over the years by the staff of Scottsdale Memorial Hospital, where patients' needs as well as those of their families are addressed by professionals.

When it opened in 1962, there were only three nurses, 10,000 residents, and the City Hospital of Scottsdale (its former name) was considered "out in the boonies." But from the beginning, excellence in patient care has been the main goal of the institution.

In 1964 the hospital was taken over by the Southern Baptist Convention of Arizona and renamed the Baptist Hospital of Scottsdale. They organized a local governing board, provided management, and launched a series of efforts to improve the hospital's operation and reputation.

The city's population explosion contributed to the hospital's improved financial condition since, for the first time, it was being fully used. Then in 1968 a series of expansions and hospital improvements began. The first two floors of the West Tower were added, increasing the bed capacity to 236 with five specialized medical departments.

Paralleling the expansion was the decision to turn the hospital over to the community. Management was assumed by a community health care facility with all assets owned by a community hospital corporation. In August 1971 the name was changed to Scottsdale Memorial Hospital.

Today Scottsdale Memorial Hospital-Osborn, 7400 East Osborn Road, has 360 acute care beds and a medical staff of more than 600 physicians and professionals in 35 specialties. Some 1,700 hospital support employees care for more than 17,000 patients annually.

SMH-Osborn is the center of the Scottsdale Memorial Health System; however, another major regional hospital—Scottsdale Memorial Hospital-North—located at 92nd Street and Shea Boulevard, opened its doors in 1984 to serve the medical needs of a projected 143,000 people in the Northeast Valley. The 60-acre campus has 120 beds, including a critical care unit, 24-hour emergency department, and four surgical suites. During the first year of operation some 250 employees worked there.

The Scottsdale Memorial system has the latest in technological advances. In July 1983 the newest technological marvel in medical imaging—the Magnetic Resonance Imaging (MRI)—was installed at SMH-Osborn. SMH is the first hospital in Arizona and one of about 24 nationwide to install the MRI, which uses magnetic waves instead of X-rays to visualize soft tissues of the body.

Other important services include an outpatient surgery center, the first free-standing hospital-sponsored center of its kind in the state, started in 1972; home health care, which provides continuity of care to discharged patients; day hospital rehabilitation for those with chronic disabling conditions; and HealthSteps, a preventive health education program for the community.

Because the Scottsdale Memorial system is committed to providing services wherever people live and need help, health centers have been established in Fountain Hills and Rio Verde. In downtown Scottsdale, adjacent to the hospital, is the Family Practice Center, which was opened in 1974 when the family practice residency program was launched.

Scottsdale Memorial Hospital-North opened its doors in January 1984 to serve the rapidly expanding northeast community.

RUSS LYON REALTY COMPANY

Russ Lyon Realty Company, the Valley of the Sun's oldest family-owned brokerage, was founded in 1947 by the late Russell A. Lyon, Sr. It has grown from a one-man enterprise to a multifaceted commercial, industrial, and residential firm projecting $300 million in sales during 1984.

The founder's youngest son, Dennis H. Lyon, president and chairman of the board, has directed the company's expansion since 1968. Russ Lyon Realty has a sales force approaching 300 sales associates working out of five Valley offices.

Russ Lyon, Sr., already had two successful careers to his credit when he and his wife, Janis, and their two young sons, Russ Jr., a prominent shopping center developer, and Dennis, a dynamic salesman who advanced through the ranks of the agency, arrived in the Valley on March 28, 1947, during orange blossom season. Lyon then proceeded to purchase a home on two and one-half acres in Scottsdale so his sons could horseback ride and explore the desert.

Russell A. Lyon, Sr., founded the realty firm that bears his name in 1947.

Lyon had been a big-band musician with Phil Spitalny's Orchestra, followed by the start of his own Russ Lyon and His Band in 1932; then he held a position with Music Corporation of America; and finally, in 1945, he formed the Russ Lyon Agency, a talent company, which he sold to a group of former MCA agents prior to moving west.

Six months after arriving in Scottsdale, he launched himself in the real estate business. Because of his personal attitudes and integrity, the venture enjoyed a healthy, rapid growth. Lyon established an organization known for quality service, total professionalism, fair play, and extreme thoroughness. Now, under the guidance of Dennis Lyon, the firm has expanded to meet the needs of the community and to maintain leadership in the real estate industry.

Russ Lyon Realty was primarily a two-office company until 1976, when expansion began with a branch office in Carefree and North Scottsdale. The expansion kept pace with the tremendous growth in the Northeast Valley. In 1980-1982 the firm expanded the Phoenix office, at 2036 East Camelback Road; the Paradise Valley branch, at 4707 East Cactus Drive; and the Carefree office, on Sundial Circle. The corporate headquarters was relocated from 68th and Camelback streets to Scottsdale Road and Lincoln Drive, where the Scottsdale branch also is located. A separate corporate headquarters has been planned and the location will be decided during 1984.

A new branch at 8711 Pinnacle Peak Road was added to the Lyon family in 1982. It is expected to double in size as Scottsdale develops to the north. There are currently 12 sales associates at this branch.

Today Russ Lyon Realty Company is directed by the son of the founder, Dennis H. Lyon, who serves as president.

"We are undergoing expansion of services other than residential," says Robert S. Cain, Jr., vice-president of residential properties. "We have opened a property management and leasing office for residential and a relocation department to accommodate the huge volume of corporate transferees, and have opened a home sales division to handle nothing but subdivision sales."

Lyon's second major division is the commercial/industrial division headed by Tom Richardson, vice-president, who has been with the firm since June 1980. Jim Tubbs, executive vice-president, has been with Russ Lyon Realty Company since 1968 and is responsible for special projects, public relations, and new-business development. Dan Hazelton is vice-president of corporate investments.

SAFARI RESORT

The Safari Resort, in 1956 the first resort to open in Scottsdale, received a $1.5-million face-lifting in 1983 that included a major reconstruction of the hotel entrance, lobby, and each of the 194 guest rooms.

The resort, renowned throughout the United States for its French Quarter Restaurant from 1960 to 1978, is located at 4611 North Scottsdale Road, across the street from Fashion Square Shopping Mall and just a few blocks from Scottsdale's Fifth Avenue shops and Main Street galleries.

When the facility opened 28 years ago it had 108 rooms and was advertised as being in "Beautiful Paradise Valley." Expansion projects in 1957, 1958, and 1960 added 86 additional rooms, an 11,000-square-foot convention center, and the French Quarter and Cabaret, where entertainers such as Rosemary Clooney, George Shearing, the DeCastro Sisters, Dennis Day, Tiny Tim, the Modernaires, the Ink Spots, and the Dukes of Dixieland performed on stage during an 18-year period. The New Orleans-style restaurant and the Safari Coffee Shop were operated by restaurateur Paul V. Shank until 1978.

Motion picture stars such as John Wayne and Bing Crosby were among the early-day celebrities who called the Safari "home" when Scottsdale was still a fledgling resort area with a population of fewer than 10,000 people.

"The Safari never suffered an unprofitable year, even during the early summers when guest traffic dwindled," says Ernie Uhlmann, who built the resort on the 11.5-acre site with his partner and operated it until 1970 when it was purchased by Ramada Inns Inc. Uhlmann still maintains an office in the upstairs executive wing of the resort hotel.

Then, in 1982, the Trammell Crow Company of Dallas, Texas, purchased the Safari Resort from Ramada Inns Inc. and initiated plans for its renovation to once again make the resort one of the city's finest.

Each of the 194 guest rooms has been upgraded; the Brown Derby Restaurant and lounge have been expanded and redesigned to offer views of the resort's courtyard pool and grounds; and the lobby area has been reconstructed.

When the Safari first opened, a doorman in native African tribal dress greeted guests at the entrance. In recreating the safari feeling, all resort employees now wear authentic safari outfits and greet arriving guests beneath a covered entryway and usher them into a modern lobby reflecting the safari character. Helping to create the new look are a zebra-striped piano, tree-trunk tables, extensive broad-leafed plantings, huge ceramic jardinieres, and a fully mirrored ceiling.

The lobby's mirrored ceiling reflects the safari theme that prevails throughout.

The new owners, who also own Wyndham Hotels and several other independent inns, are the nation's largest developer of commercial, industrial, and retail properties. Charles R. Paul, senior partner in Trammell Crow's Phoenix office, is operating the Safari "as a unique downtown Scottsdale resort hotel" within the Ramada Inns' franchise.

E. Sue Russell has been general manager of the Safari since June 1984. She has been with the Scottsdale Hilton for the past eight years, serving for five of those years as vice-president of finance (as well as of the Denver Airport Hilton), and for the past three years (and currently) as its general manager.

The Safari Resort, home of the Brown Derby Restaurant and Lounge, has been a popular Scottsdale spot for travelers, celebrities, and local residents alike.

PAUL'S HARDWARE

When Paul Dauwalder was discharged from the service following World War II, the Indiana farm boy was not certain what business opportunities were available in Arizona, but he was soon to find out. His parents had moved to Glendale during the war years, leaving the Indiana farm behind.

Dauwalder soon became associated with O'Malley's Lumber Company as a venetian blind installer, and later worked in the hardware department and in the lumberyard for over nine years before deciding to purchase his own hardware store. At the time Scottsdale had three hardware and lumber businesses. Dauwalder purchased the already existing Scottsdale Hardware Store at Thomas and Scottsdale roads in 1956, a store that had been operating for some 10 years.

Within two years the venture had outgrown its location, and Dauwalder moved to a larger facility at 3028 North Scottsdale Road, where Warren TV & Appliance is now located. The store thrived there for the next eight years, until still more square footage was needed. Dauwalder then leased what had been Scottsdale's fifth U.S. Post Office, 7131 Fourth Street, which had been built in 1958 by Earl Shipp, and moved in in 1967.

Today Dauwalder's faithful customers include winter visitors who return year after year to set up housekeeping for the season. "We have everything from nails to kitchen towels and pot holders, from water heaters to lawn mowers, and a wide variety of tools for the home owner as well as for professionals," says Dauwalder.

Paul's Hardware joined the True Value® family in 1970, added a warehouse and enlarged the parking lot in 1971, and incorporated the business with Paul Dauwalder as president; son Don Dauwalder, vice-president; and Paul's wife, Margaret, secretary/treasurer of the corporation in 1972. Then, in 1973, they opened a second store in Fountain Hills.

The firm, with 30 full- and part-time employees, now enjoys gross sales of more than two million dollars a year. To maintain this excellent record, the Dauwalders emphasize customer satisfaction. "If a customer leaves our store and goes to another store to find something he needs, the chances are 50-50 that the next time he needs something he will go to the competition first," says Paul Dauwalder. "Our pledge is that if we don't have it, we will get it."

Although the elder Dauwalder has no plans to retire, if he should decide to take a long vacation, the business would be left in the capable hands of his son Don, who first began working for the company when he was eight years old—barely tall enough to push a broom and stock the shelves. Two other sons, Fred, an engineer with Garrett Corporation, and David, a secondary-education instructor in Michigan, also worked in the family-owned enterprise while growing up.

Paul, who has been married to Margaret for 38 years, has been honored for his service to the California-Pacific-Southwest Hardware Association, a tradition being carried on by Don Dauwalder, who currently serves on the board of directors.

Scottsdale's fifth post office (below), built in 1958 and leased by the postal service for nine years, was turned into Paul's Scottsdale Hardware in 1967 (bottom), and has been operated by Paul Dauwalder for the past 17 years at 7131 Fourth Street in downtown Scottsdale.

EL CHORRO LODGE

A Valley landmark since 1934, El Chorro Lodge was originally built as a satellite facility for the Judson School. It became one of the area's oldest dining establishments in 1937 when it was purchased by Janet and Mark Gruber, who operated it for the next 36 years.

The Lodge, located at 5550 Lincoln Drive, situated in much the same terrain as 50 years ago, is now owned by two former 20-year employees of the Grubers, Joe and Evie Miller, who purchased the well-known restaurant in 1973. The original intent to make the Lodge into a girls' school by George A. Judson never materialized; however, several boys lived at the residence and rode their horses each day to the main campus on Mockingbird Lane.

Joe Miller recalls that the early resort days along Lincoln Drive consisted of the Camelback Inn, a short distance to the west, and El Chorro Lodge. Guests would walk or ride their horses over from Camelback to the Lodge at night. "It was different then because our customers were mainly tourists," he says. "There weren't too many people around this area and it wasn't until Mountain Shadows opened in 1958 that business began to pick up. In those days Camelback was completely American Plan, but guests usually came over to the Lodge at least one night during their stay."

Joe Miller came to the Valley from Seattle, Washington, in 1951 and started working at Camelback before being persuaded by the Grubers to join the El Chorro staff in 1952. At that time there were about 20 employees, and today the Millers employ 104. "In 1952 we served three meals a day and had one cook who helped wash the pots, pans, and dishes," Joe Miller recalls. "If we served 25 people at noon that was considered a big lunch."

The bar of the El Chorro Lodge in 1938. Originally built as a satellite facility for the Judson School, it is one of the area's oldest dining establishments.

The numbers have changed considerably since the 1950s. Today, with Sunday brunch from 9 a.m. to 3 p.m. and dinner from 6 to 11 p.m., the restaurant serves over 1,000 people. "We do as much business during the month of March as we used to do the entire year," Miller says. "At Sunday brunch we serve two meals a minute and all are cooked to order. We never prepare ahead."

During the years the specialties of the house have remained pretty much the same, with rack of lamb, chateaubriand, pan-fried chicken, and eggs Benedict having the reputation of the "best in town." Perhaps the most famous delicacy of the house is the sticky buns served at all three meals.

Joe Miller has been involved in community life for decades. For the past seven years he has served on the board of the Scottsdale Boys' Club, and for the past six years on the Phoenix 100 board. In addition, he is a member of the Scottsdale Charros and the Verde Vaqueros and never misses one of their trail rides.

Over the years the Lodge has maintained its cozy atmosphere of home dining. When the Grubers purchased the white stucco buildings with their red tile roofs, they built a kitchen and 12 guest cottages, of which three remain today.

Although today's guests do not arrive by horseback and tie their horses to the Lodge's hitching post, they still enjoy the the same excellent food, friendly service, and unforgettable views of Camelback and Mummy mountains as they sip cool beverages on the Lodge patio surrounded by tall palm trees amidst natural desert flora.

JUDSON SCHOOL

The white tower with the red tile roof of the Judson School has long been a landmark of Arizona's oldest independent college preparatory school, founded in 1928 by George A. Judson of Michigan.

A former superintendent of the Phoenix Osborn School District, he believed that the state needed a school where boys from colder climates could receive a well-rounded education amidst sunshine in the healthful Valley weather.

The school, located at 6704 North Mockingbird Lane, Paradise Valley, opened in 1928 with eight boys attending classes in one schoolhouse with a dining room, library, health center, two tennis courts, a baseball field, polo field, water tower, and stables on the 40-acre campus situated at the foot of Mummy Mountain. Judson was aided financially in his venture by John C. Lincoln and other leading Valley families.

Famed Camelback Mountain is the backdrop for Judson's 55-acre-ranch campus. The original adobe buildings with their red tile trim and mature landscaping are familiar landmarks to generations of children the world over.

Henry and Barbara Wick welcome students and families from all over the world to their busy home on campus where all national celebrations are held.

Students those first few years came from New York, Detroit, Cleveland, and the state of Kansas. Each fall Judson would personally escort the youths to the Valley, starting with a small group at the New York Central Railroad, gathering more boys in Chicago, and transferring the group to the Golden State Liner bound for Phoenix.

In 1938 Judson was joined by a young Yale graduate, Henry C. Wick III, who now is president and director of Judson. Wick has been dedicated to the school since that time, with the exception of three years during World War II when he served as a captain in the U.S. Army.

When Judson became ill and retired in 1946, Wick succeeded him. At the time there were 40 boys at Judson. Ten years later Wick took a daring step and opened Judson's door to girls. Today there are approximately 500 students, with 350 of those boarders from 38 states and 24 foreign countries. Of this number, 160 are girls in grades one through 12.

A satellite school had been built a few miles west on Lincoln Drive (now El Chorro Lodge) with the idea of making it into the girls' school, but the plan never materialized. Instead, the first girls' dormitory was built in 1956 adjoining the home of Henry and his wife, Barbara Wick, who serves as the school's admissions director. Since that time, five acres on the north side of Indian Bend Road have become a residential complex for upper school girls, an area that is off-limits to male students.

The school has grown and prospered through the years and is recognized for its small classes, academic excellence, and extracurricular acitivities. Polo has given way to football, the staff has grown from 40 to 180, and some 50 horses are kept in the stables. Students also compete in 12 sports, including tennis, golf, football, basketball, and soccer.

In addition to preparing students for admission to well-known universities across the country, Judson is proud of its ability to introduce foreign students to the American way of life—which contributes to a better understanding between all nations.

English and western riding remains one of the all-time popular sports on campus.

RURAL/METRO CORPORATION

Scottsdale's fire department is a unique and world-renowned service operated by Rural/Metro Corporation, which is the nation's largest employee-owned contract fire service.

Rural/Metro was founded in 1948 by Lou Witzeman, a 23-year-old University of Arizona journalism school graduate who had moved to Phoenix to take a newspaper job and purchased a home in the suburbs. When a nearby home burned to the ground because no fire service responded, Witzeman decided to start a fire department.

He first tried unsuccessfully to form a fire district; then he attempted to form a co-op but abandoned the idea when neighbors failed to meet financial pledges; and finally he decided to form his own fire company. Witzeman made a $900 down payment on a fire truck, hired three men, and charged subscribing residents $12 per year for fire protection.

Rural/Metro was providing limited protection to the Scottsdale area when the city incorporated in 1951. At that time the Scottsdale School District owned a small trailer equipped with a tank of water and a pump, which was the community's only fire protection equipment. Manned by volunteers, the fire trailer was dispatched to meet the men of Rural/Metro at the scene of a fire. Among the early-day volunteers was Mort Kimsey, who became Scottsdale's first mayor. As a volunteer, Kimsey was well acquainted with the capabilities of Rural/Metro.

After the city incorporated, Mayor Kimsey asked Witzeman to consider a fire service contract with Scottsdale. Upon approval by the first city council, Rural/Metro became the city's official fire department and purchased a lot at the northwest corner of Second Street and Brown Avenue where it erected a building consisting of two small wings separated by a truck bay large enough for two emergency fire vehicles. Under the terms of the first contract, the city paid Rural/Metro $300 a month for protection and the city received the services of two full-time fire fighters, a large group of paid, on-call reservists, and two pieces of fire apparatus. For $30 a month more, Scottsdale rented the south wing which became the city's first city hall.

Rural/Metro has served Scottsdale ever since. The department has grown to 35 stations in Arizona, including five in Scottsdale, a fleet of 140 vehicles in Arizona and 165 nationwide, and is recognized for its innovations. The service has pioneered by using city employees as trained auxiliary fire fighters, writing progressive fire prevention and sprinkler codes, constructing its own fire equipment, using large-diameter fire hose, and painting trucks a safer lime-yellow color.

Today Rural/Metro is the largest contract fire service in the nation and serves 20 percent of Arizona's population in addition to portions of Tennessee, New Mexico, and Texas. It offers not only fire service but ambulance and security services and alarm installation and monitoring.

When Witzeman retired in 1981, he sold the firm to his employees. Ron Butler, a 16-year Rural/Metro veteran, became chief executive officer. He believes much of the company's growth and progress in evolving a system that delivers fire service for approximately half the national average cost might have been accomplished only in a community such as Scottsdale.

"Scottsdale, through its growth from 2,500 people to more than 100,000, has managed to keep an attitude that creates and welcomes innovation," Butler says. "Not only the city's political officials and administrators but the electorate have consistently supported innovation—thus making Scottsdale a prosperous American city."

In the 1950s this fleet of Rural/Metro fire trucks served a growing township. Fourteen full- and part-time fire fighters and the chief are shown in front of the first station, at 120 South Brown Street.

Rural/Metro was founded in 1948 by Lou Witzeman (left), who retired as chief executive in 1981. The current board chairman, Ron Butler, is on the right. ©S. Duncan, 1984.

BUCK SAUNDERS TRADING POST AND GALLERY

The first art show in Scottsdale took place on February 5, 1950, at the Buck Saunders Trading Post and Gallery on Brown Avenue for a man who would one day become one of the most sought-after artists in the world, Ted De Grazia.

The show that winter day more than 30 years ago was an adventure for the gallery owners, Buck and Leo Saunders, and the artist Ted De Grazia. It was decided to repaint the walls of the gallery the night before the show with colors selected by De Grazia to complement the paintings that he had brought for the exhibit.

At this time the population of Scottsdale was little more than 2,000 people. To everyone's amazement about 1,500 people showed up to view the art works of this controversial artist. The restaurants ran out of food, and the Pink Pony, not then using an ice-making machine, ran out of ice. Though the show was scheduled to open at 2 o'clock, the ladies from Elizabeth Arden's Maine Chance Spa asked if they could come early to fit in with the routine at the salon. They came, they saw, and they left with many watercolors to give the show a good and surprising start.

When the doors finally opened at the announced time, the people began to arrive in droves. Since no one had thought to provide a guest book, a stenographer's note pad was substituted. Its pages contain the names of people from many areas, including New York, Indiana, Utah, and Canada, in addition to people from Phoenix and other Arizona towns. When the doors closed at the advertised hour of 8 o'clock, some $1,500 in paintings had been sold—a large sum for that time, since the watercolors started at $20 and the most expensive oil was offered at about $400.

On March 5, 1950, the gallery held its second successful art show. Paintings by Taos Indian artist Pop Chalee and her husband, Navajo Indian artist Ed Lee Natay, were shown. Ms. Chalee's work is widely known and her paintings are in both private and public collections throughout the world. The gallery still shows her paintings, along with the works of many other American Indian artists including Harrison Begay, Robert Redbird, and Diane O'Leary.

In 1972 the Brown Avenue gallery, which had opened on March 1, 1949, was closed, but Saunders and his wife, Leo, are still very much in business at the Buck Saunders Trading Post and Gallery, 2724 North Scottsdale Road. This location was opened in 1952 as a frame shop and began to show paintings about 1963. This gallery can only be described as a mini-museum and a treasure trove for collectors. Here De Grazia, who passed away in 1982, lives on in the memory of both Leo and Buck Saunders, who were his friends and confidants for more than 30 years. At De Grazia's request, Buck Saunders wrote the section entitled "The Man and His Art" in the book *The World of De Grazia* by Harry Redl.

Shortly after the art shows of the 1950s, Saunders decided to add art supplies to the trading post's inventory of gifts, prints, and paintings, since the nearest source of supplies was 10 miles away in Phoenix. The customers included such well-known artists as Marjorie Thomas, William Schimmel, Phil Curtis, Francis Beaugereau, and Mark Coomer. For many years Schimmel showed his paintings with the gallery.

A native of Virginia, Saunders has had an interest in art since doing his first oil painting at age nine. In the early part of a 23-year career in civil engineering, he worked in architecture and did many renderings, in various media, of proposed structures. For two years he was secretary of the Riverside, California, Fine Arts Guild, and after moving to Arizona in 1947, he served three years as president of the Arizona Artist Guild. He came to Arizona as a civilian construction engineer with the U.S. Army Corps of Engineers in charge of the Corps' various projects in the state, which later included the construction of the first section of the Phoenix Veterans Hospital.

Over the years Saunders has talked to many people who were interested in purchasing art. His advice has always been, "Buy it if you like it, can afford it, and want to live with it. Then, should you have to dispose of it and can get more than you paid for it, consider the profit as a bonus to your enjoyment. Do not, for the average purchaser, buy for investment only."

Buck and Leobarda Saunders Trading Post and Gallery has been located at 2724 North Scottsdale Road since 1952. Originally opened as a frame shop, it began to show paintings about 1963.

THE PONDEROSA LUMBER CO.

A.C. Mason (right), co-founder, chairman of the board, and president until 1984, and his son Dave, who is now president of The Ponderosa Lumber Co.

The Ponderosa Lumber Co. opened its doors on April 1, 1965, at 6425 East Thomas Road with a total of five employees. Since that time it has prospered with the addition of True Value Homes and the Ponderosa Truss Manufacturing Plant into a $10-million business.

The three founders, all employed at the time by O'Malley Scottsdale Lumber Company, were A.C. Mason, the majority stockholder who served as president and chairman of the board until 1984; Bon W. "Buck" Logan, vice-president of sales; and Frank Hennessey, secretary/treasurer. In 1970 Hennessey retired and sold his shares of the expanding enterprise to Mason and Logan. Logan now is secretary/treasurer while Mason's son Dave, who has worked full time at the Ponderosa for the past 10 years, is the president.

The three-acre site of the full-service lumber company was first leased and in 1973 purchased from Mr. and Mrs. L.M. Hamman, owners of the Hamman-McFarland Lumber Company, a venture they had operated for five years.

Founder Mason first became interested in lumber when he was old enough to take wood shop at school. "I loved the smell of sawdust and I loved wood and the things I could make out of it," he recalls. Although a native of Oklahoma, he was reared in Miami, Arizona, where his father had been an electrician in the mines. He graduated from Miami High School but his studies at Arizona State University were interrupted when he joined the U.S. Navy during World War II.

Mason's associate, Logan, came to the Valley in 1949 from Michigan via Indiana. He had worked for both the Reed Lumber Company and the Ray Lumber Company for 13 years prior to joining O'Malley's. During World War II, Logan served as a fighter pilot.

With these two men at the helm, the Ponderosa prospered along with Scottsdale's building boom. The contractor-oriented lumberyard, geared to the custom home builder, is the only full-service lumberyard remaining in Scottsdale. In addition to the 5,000-square-foot western-style concrete block building where the hardware store and lumber business are located, the prehung door plant is housed in a second facility constructed in 1967.

The truss-rafter manufacturing plant, started at the southwest corner of the lumberyard in 1966, has since outgrown its space and was moved in 1979 to new quarters on 10 acres in Chandler. There, near the I-10 Freeway and a Southern Pacific spur line, better accessibility and increased capabilities have allowed the truss-fabricating plant to grow to the capability of a $4-million-volume business.

Then, in the spring of 1973, Ponderosa entered into the summer home market and built the first True Value Home model on acreage next to the lumber company. Components for the prefabricated home are all manufactured by the Ponderosa and include wall sections, roof trusses, prehung doors, and plumbing walls. The first year 30 units were built and sold at an average of $5,000 per unit. Now, the division is capable of fabricating 750 houses a year at Ponderosa facilities.

In the next decade The Ponderosa Lumber Co. looks forward to a bright future with second-generation Masons at its helm. In addition to Dave, another son, Steve, who retired from the U.S. Navy in May 1984, has joined the work force; daughter Meg Bushard, the eldest of the five Mason children, works part time in the accounting department. Two other sons not associated with the business are Richard, a dentist, and Mark, Steve's twin brother, of Seattle.

WESTERN DEVCOR INC.

Western Devcor Inc., a Scottsdale-based development firm, has taken the lead in changing the look of downtown Scottsdale through the development of the Scottsdale Financial Center at Scottsdale and Indian School roads. Western Devcor, active in commercial and residential real estate development in Arizona and Texas, recently announced the start of Scottsdale Financial Center II, the second phase of the project.

The multiphased, high-profile brick and reflective-glass project is consistent with Western Devcor's philosophy of high-quality development at a prime location. Devcor's president, Walter W. Rector, believes that Scottsdale Financial Center is an important factor in the commercial rejuvenation of Scottsdale's downtown area.

"Our analysis of market trends indicated the downtown area, confined primarily to small shops and local businesses, offered an extraordinary opportunity for a major development," Rector says, "city planners, searching for ways to improve year-round economic stability, agreed."

Western Devcor's headquarters currently is located on the third floor of the completed first-phase $22-million structure located on the northwest corner of Scottsdale and Indian School roads, where a supermarket, the Ranch House hamburger stand, and the Town Pump service station once stood.

The second-phase, 150,000-square-foot, three-story brick and reflective-glass building, under construction on the northeast corner of Scottsdale and Indian School roads, may well be the most historically significant location in the city. Although no marker is placed there, it was in this location that Chaplain Winfield Scott, the town's founder, built his home and 100 years ago harvested such crops as oranges, lemons, grapefruit, grapes, raisins, apricots, peaches, pears, plums, figs, almonds, and peanuts.

Western Devcor officers are (left to right) Walter W. Rector, president; Robert W. Lees, vice-president; and Robert G. Mayfield, executive vice-president. Photo by Koppes.

The complete development plan calls for two more structures to be built at a future date by joint-development partners, Western Devcor and Fidelity National Title Insurance Company, a subsidiary of Security Financial Corporation of Scottsdale.

Western Devcor Inc. was formed in 1982 by Rector and two business associates. Before that, each of Devcor's founders was active in real estate development in Arizona and the Southwest. Rector began his mortgage banking and development business in 1975 with Community Development Corporation and Community Financial Corporation in Scottsdale. Robert G. Mayfield, Devcor's executive vice-president, joined the Bellamah Corporation in 1971, developing commercial projects in New Mexico, Colorado, and Arizona. Bob Lees, the third member of Devcor's founding team and a vice-president, was with Ernest W. Hahn for 10 years. Lees, a CPA , was president of Ernest W. Hahn Inc., one of the largest regional shopping center developers in the world.

The enterprise, which has been based in Scottsdale since its inception, concentrates on the development of large class-A office and mixed-use commercial developments in prime metropolitan locations, and on garden and mid-rise multifamily projects Devcor currently has projects valued at more than $300 million under way.

Among tenants in the Financial Center is Security Savings and Loan, one of the state's leading financial institutions, which relocated its headquarters from Tucson to Scottsdale to be closer to the state's area of growth and development. Others include the law firm of O'Connor, Cavanagh, Anderson, Westover, Killingsworth & Beshears, the Scottsdale Commercial Bank, the Phoenix regional offices of Conti Commodity Services Inc., Manufacturer's Hanover, and Fidelity National Title Insurance Company.

SCOTTSDALE PLUMBING COMPANY, INC.

The Scottsdale Plumbing Company, started in 1946 by Art and Mildred Bratzel, has been operated by family members since that time. Today it is owned by their three grandchildren, who are carrying on the family tradition of service excellence to the community.

In 1984 Scottsdale Plumbing, 7501 East Osborn Road, took on a new identity when the Covington brothers, Ed and Michael, and their sister, Linda, purchased a DIAL ONE™ franchise, which in the Phoenix-Scottsdale area includes 35 trades and services that meet strict standards of customer satisfaction.

The firm has grown over the past 38 years from a husband-and-wife operation to 20 full-time employees and eight plumbers, and from one 1940s Ford pickup truck to a fleet of seven streamlined vans and three pickup trucks.

Art Bratzel had only one 1940 vintage pickup truck when he started the firm in 1946.

In the beginning the Bratzels lived in a three-bedroom apartment over the plumbing store at 42 West Second Street in Scottsdale. Mildred answered the phone, sold parts, and kept the books while Art serviced the plumbing needs of the growing community. In 1949 their son, Mel Covington, joined the enterprise. He worked days in the plumbing store and nights at the Rusty Spur Tavern, which he owned for a time in the 1950s. "Basically, Mel ran the business and Art was the plumber," Ed Covington recalls. "Almost all the sewers in the city were installed by Art and then he hooked up all the houses to the new sewer system."

The Bratzels' contribution to the city's early growth was significant. Art installed and inspected plumbing work in Scottsdale before the city had its own inspection department; wrote, administered, and graded tests in 1959 to Scottsdale's first building inspector; and served 25 years on the city's Plumbing and Mechanical Advisory Board, 11 years as chairman.

Scottsdale Plumbing Company, 7501 East Osborn Road, has been serving the Scottsdale community since 1946.

Mildred Bratzel, who had attended the Little Red Schoolhouse and Scottsdale High School, was the city's first councilwoman, elected in 1958. That same year she was named Business Woman of the Year by the Scottsdale Association of Business and Professional Women. She served as president of the auxiliary of the State Association of Plumbing Contractors and as president of the Toastmistress Club.

Through the years Scottsdale Plumbing relocated from its Second Street address to 3711 North 75th Street, and finally to the new two-story, 8,000-square-foot Bratzel Building at Osborn and 75th streets in 1965. Here the largest inventory of plumbing supplies, including 24-karat gold, brass, and pewter bathroom fixtures, can be found. "We carry all brand names and have the largest inventory of parts and supplies in the Valley," says Covington.

The old days may be gone, but they are not forgotten. One reminder for Ed, president of Scottsdale Plumbing, and Mike, the secretary/treasurer, is the recent discovery of a yellowed service ticket hidden on the back shelf of the company's safe. One Saturday morning in 1957 their grandfather, Art Bratzel, had replaced a washer on a leaky faucet at the Cheney Ranch on Mockingbird Lane, charging time-and-a-half for the job. The bill came to $7.50, but was lost and has never been collected.

ARIZONA CONFERENCE OF SEVENTH-DAY ADVENTISTS

The first Seventh-day Adventist Church in Arizona was established in 1890 at Third and Pierce streets in Phoenix with about 20 members. Since that time the church has grown to 55 congregations and 8,000 members statewide. Established in 1902, the Arizona Conference administrative offices are now located at 13405 North Scottsdale Road, adjacent to its educational boarding school campus.

That school was established after the church acquired 720 acres, then known as Thunderbird Field II, from the U.S. Department of Health, Education, and Welfare on July 2, 1953. The school was named Thunderbird Adventist Academy and averages 250 students annually.

In March 1965 the Arizona Conference Corporation, at the time headed by D.C. Butherus, president, gave 201 acres of land to the City of Scottsdale for an airport, with the academy retaining perpetual use of the airstrip to train its students, some of whom are serving the church as missionary pilots. In order to receive federal assistance in the development of the airport, the city made arrangements to purchase the acreage from the Arizona Conference for $750,000. In July 1966 the Arizona Conference made a cash donation to the City of Scottsdale in the sum of $750,000.

Later, as a tribute to the conference and its president, the Scottsdale Municipal Airport's main entrance street was named Butherus Drive after Butherus, who had spearheaded the exchange of land. The Arizona Conference still owns nearly 80 acres, which comprise the school campus and the conference's new headquarters building.

The administrative office building was dedicated by president E. Frank Sherrill on September 25, 1983. The facility, which reflects a southwestern theme, was designed by Charles R. Schiffner, an architect with the Frank Lloyd Wright Foundation (Arizona), Taliesin Associated Architects, in the form of a cross. In the center of the cross is a vaulted ceiling atrium that serves as a reception area and allows natural light to pour through the skylight.

Early-morning desert hues are used throughout the center, from the carpeting to the lighted stained-glass pillars. Dr. Jeanne Bengtsson was the interior architect. The center includes a board room; a seminar room; a communications center complete with an offset press and other in-house printing facilities servicing the entire state; the departments of education, youth, and health activities; community services; and the Adventist Book Center and Health Food Store, which features vegetarian products and is open to the public. A staff lunch room is also included.

From this center the Seventh-day Adventist churches throughout the state are service-oriented and have distinguished themselves by supplying assistance to the needy in the form of food and clothing; developing the Five-Day Plan to Stop Smoking; providing Christian education through their parochial school system; providing disaster and food emergency relief preparedness programs; initiating Pathfinder Clubs, an organization comparable to the Boy Scout movement; advocating healthful living; and providing medical services, retirement centers, hospitals, and training centers in 184 countries.

The new Arizona Conference of Seventh-day Adventists headquarters in North Scottsdale was designed by Charles R. Schiffner with the Frank Lloyd Wright Foundation at Taliesin. The building reflects a southwestern theme and encompasses the Adventist Book Center and Health Food Store, which are open to the public.

SCOTTSDALE COMMUNITY COLLEGE

Scottsdale Community College opened its doors in September 1970 with 948 students, 20 full-time faculty, and 30 visiting staff members.

This was the beginning that has brought the college to what it is today, a respected institution of higher learning serving more than 7,500 students of Scottsdale and the communities of Paradise Valley, Fountain Hills, Carefree, Cave Creek, the northern part of Tempe, eastern Phoenix, and the Indian communities of Salt River and Fort McDowell.

Originally the college was not at its present location at 9000 East Chaparral, but functioned as an extension of Mesa Community College with classes held in a rented former church building at 4208 North 82nd Street as well as at Scottsdale High School. To avoid interference with high school activities, most college classes were held in the evening.

Scottsdale College is one of seven colleges in the Maricopa Community Colleges District, which was formed in 1960. With the growth of northeast Phoenix and Scottsdale, it was decided to establish a college in Scottsdale in 1967. The college is unique in its location on 160 acres of land obtained through a 99-year lease agreement with the Salt River Pima-Maricopa Indian Community and the Bureau of Indian Affairs.

In October 1968 a bond election was passed to provide funds for the first-phase construction of SCC, and a search was begun for an executive dean to guide the new institution. Dr. Marion Donaldson became the first executive dean, opening an administrative office in the leased church building on August 18, 1969. Sixteen portable facilities were moved on campus during the summer of 1970 from the Mesa, Glendale, and Phoenix campuses, and one large metal building was constructed.

The first phase of the permanent buildings was completed in 1972. This included the science building, completed in the fall of 1971, and the student center, library, gymnasium, and technology buildings, completed in the spring of 1972. A 350-seat performing arts center was added in 1978. Here concerts, plays, recitals, lectures, and musicals are performed. The 17,000-square-foot music building was added in May 1981 to include an instrumental rehearsal hall, choral rehearsal and recital hall, ensemble room, and individual practice rooms.

As a comprehensive community college, SCC offers a wide spectrum of university transfer, occupational, and community service programs and offers three separate associate degrees. In the past few years the college has broadened its occupational curriculum and now offers more opportunities for students to prepare for careers that do not require four-year degrees.

The busy campus of Scottsdale Community College. The school offers a wide spectrum of university transfer, occupational, and community service programs.

A variety of technologies, human services, and health and business programs, such as interior design, equine science, tribal management, electronics/microprocessor technology, and nursing and business information systems, are offered at Scottsdale Community College. Programs are added or deleted in accordance with the needs of students, the community, business, and industry.

Under the leadership of Dr. Arthur W. DeCabooter, the college has grown and prospered. Dr. DeCabooter, the president, came to Scottsdale from Black Hawk College in Kewanee, Illinois, in 1977. He has developed an effective team approach among administrative staff and instituted both short- and long-term planning efforts that involve faculty, staff, and students in charting the course of SCC through the '80s and '90s.

IVERSON'S INDIAN ARTS AND CRAFTS STUDIO

North Dakota farmer Elmer Iverson first came to Scottsdale 24 years ago to spend the winter and "take it easy," but before he knew it he had become fascinated with Indian jewelry and crafts and became a trader, making frequent trips to the Zuni reservation in Gallup, New Mexico.

Prior to opening Iverson's Indian Arts and Crafts Studio in the Stetson Plaza Building, 7120 Sixth Avenue, in Studio 20 more than a decade ago, he bought Indian jewelry wholesale from the reservation and sold it to other Valley dealers.

Iverson first became interested in the Native American arts when a neighbor invited him to accompany him on several trips to the Zuni reservation near Gallup. However, the second time he went there with the same friend, the police drove the pair off the territory and told them never to return because the friend had not renewed his bond. Iverson, who had done nothing wrong, then decided he would apply for a license, become bonded, and do business with his newfound friends. At that time a license cost $1,000 a year for unlimited trips, while now a buyer pays $20 a day.

In the beginning, he would trade used furniture and other objects the Indians needed for squash-blossom necklaces and other Indian crafts. Now, however, the buying is done on a cash-only basis. Iverson still deals directly with the Indians who have known and trusted him for many years.

The Indians still sell from their homes, and not from a sophisticated shop or factory as many people might think. A good percentage of the Zuni people are involved in jewelry making as a livelihood.

Through the years Iverson's son, Paul, has become a designer of jewelry using the same native gemstones that he first watched the Indian silversmiths combine into beautiful necklaces, rings, and bracelets when he was only 14 years old. He now creates one-of-a-kind handcrafted bracelets, rings, necklaces, and bola ties using lapis, coral, jet, mother-of-pearl, and turquoise inlaid in unique designs with silver. Paul, who lives and works in Cornville near Sedona, is expected to take over the shop when his father retires.

The majority of Iverson's clientele are local. "I'm off Fifth Avenue so that we get very few tourists," Iverson says. "Our reputation is built around authentic Indian arts and crafts for realistic prices."

The beautifully arranged exhibits of pottery include work by the Zuni, Santa Clara, Zia, Hopi, Maricopa, Acoma, and Jemez peoples. The shop walls are adorned with Navajo rugs and Navajo sand paintings, and wall cases display colorful Hopi kachinas and other artifacts. The customer can find the most intricate designs of needlepoint, pettipoint, nugget, inlay, or liquid silver created by such well-known native silversmiths as Dennis Edaakie, particularly noted for his reversible pendants and bola tie originals.

A trademark that has been with Iverson since he first opened a studio across the street from the present location 14 years ago is "Charlie," who spends his days sitting resplendent in a chieftain's headdress fitted over his handcarved wooden head. "He has sat outside my shop ever since I've had it," Iverson says. "I began right across the street where the antique store now stands, in one of the original developments along Sixth Avenue."

Iverson returns to his 3,500-acre ranch in North Dakota that he and a son operate together in the summertime and flies back to Scottsdale twice during the summer to restock the shelves. Back on the farm he raises sunflowers, wheat, and barley in order to subsidize his wintertime hobby of buying and selling beautiful native crafts at reasonable prices.

The Iversons' son, Paul, a designer of jewelry using native gemstones, is expected to take over the shop when his father retires.

Mr. and Mrs. Elmer Iverson are owners of Iverson's Indian Arts and Crafts Studio, located in Studio 20 in the Stetson Plaza Building.

MARKLAND PROPERTIES, INC.

Although part of a corporation chartered in 1670, Markland Properties established its roots in Scottsdale in 1977. From the beginning, the company was destined to become one of the largest land developers in Scottsdale, developing what are considered two of the city's most historic properties—Scottsdale Ranch and Gainey Ranch.

The 1,119-acre Scottsdale Ranch, located between 96th and 112th streets, was an original part of the McCormick Ranch. It was purchased in April 1978 from AL&C Realty Holdings Corporation, the original McCormick Ranch developer. Overseeing the land purchase was James M. Kilday, president and chief executive officer of Markland, who guided the development of the multimillion-dollar residential community of 4,064 homes centered around a 42-acre water-retention lake that is part of the Indian Bend Flood Control System. Lake Serena is used by Scottsdale Ranch residents for leisure boating and sailing.

The main property presently being developed is the 640-acre Gainey Ranch, which was purchased from the Daniel C. Gainey estate in October 1980. The Gainey family established the second Arabian horse property in Scottsdale's history. Eighty acres are still retained by the Gainey heirs and are used as a working Arabian ranch. In addition, the developers have preserved the Gainey residence, built in 1958, with its 10-foot-tall doorways, marble and brass appointments, and extensive use of glass throughout. The home is expected to be incorporated into a private club for residents of Gainey Ranch.

Golfers will face a spectacular mountain view when approaching the green from the right side of the fairway on the fifth hole of the Arroyo Nine, one of the three nines that comprise the Gainey Ranch Golf Course.

The Gainey Ranch ultimately will include a permanent population of 5,000 people; 2,000 luxury homes; a 27-hole championship golf course; and private golf and tennis clubs—all within walking distance of a town center comprised of luxury offices and retail shops and a 450-room resort hotel.

Unique to the Gainey is the state-of-the-art Gainey Water Reclamation Plant, which developers constructed at a cost of $4 million on 5.3 acres at the corner of Scottsdale and Mountain View roads and donated to the city. Markland in turn purchases the recycled water back from the city to irrigate the 27-hole golf course by a sophisticated computerized irrigation system that is designed to conserve water.

Kilday, a certified public accountant, came to the Valley in 1973 seeking real estate development opportunities. In 1977 he started Markland Properties, Inc., a subsidiary of Markborough Properties, Ltd., a wholly owned subsidiary of the Hudson's Bay Company of Canada, the oldest chartered trading company in the world. By 1984 Markland had assets in excess of $100 million and projected property values on the Gainey Ranch worth in excess of one billion dollars.

"The Gainey Ranch will be the Southwest's most luxurious resort development," Kilday says. "We are referring to it as the living resort. It's resort living at its finest. Everything is designed to be comfortable, secure, luxurious, and recreation-oriented, including golf, tennis, croquet, and five miles of bicycle, pedestrian, and jogging trails."

The Daniel C. Gainey residence in Scottsdale, built in 1958, is currently being used as the executive offices of Markland Properties.

W.A. KRUEGER CO.

The W.A. Krueger Co. of Scottsdale, one of the top 10 printing companies in the nation with revenues exceeding $216 million, celebrated its 50th anniversary in 1984.

From the moment of its inception in Milwaukee, Wisconsin, in 1934, Krueger was projected by its founders, William A. Krueger, Robert A. Klaus, and Donald C. Brock, to become a major national printing concern. The firm today—specializing in high quality, multicolor web offset lithography—produces some of the nation's best known newsweekly, special interest, and business magazines; top quality, high color content books and educational texts; and is a virtual "Who's Who" in the prestigious mail order catalog market.

One of the fastest growing companies in the industry and among the industry's best financial performers, Krueger offers a comprehensive service including composition, color preparation, printing, binding, and distribution by some 2,400 employees in its six manufacturing centers strategically located in the United States. They are in Phoenix, Arizona; Brookfield and New Berlin, Wisconsin; Jonesboro, Arkansas; Senatobia, Mississippi; and Pontiac, Illinois.

President and chief executive officer Jack W. Fowler in the pressroom of the Krueger/ Phoenix plant, where Arizona Highways *is printed.*

Having completed a modern magazine and commercial printing headquarters division in Brookfield, Wisconsin, in 1959, Krueger began integrating its expansion plan with the opening of the Phoenix plant, 2808 West Palm Lane, in 1962. In this plant the firm prints the renowned *Arizona Highways* monthly magazine, which it began printing in 1950 when Krueger still had but one Wisconsin plant. The Phoenix plant, esteemed for its catalog production, also is recognized as a leader in color reproduction and for advanced computerized drafting and mask production prepress equipment.

Company founders Krueger and Klaus, now consultants to the board, consider the 1950 attainment of the *Arizona Highways* contract a turning point in the company's history. "That was the moment we began to build a national reputation for our color lithography," recalls Krueger.

Krueger's rapid expansion after 1962—when it merged with a major bookbinding company, Brock & Rankin, and created in New Berlin, Wisconsin, one of the largest book production centers in the United States—brought about the decision in 1973 to move corporate management and administrative personnel from Wisconsin to Scottsdale, Arizona. Here, the corporate headquarters is located at 7301 East Helm Drive in the prestigious Scottsdale Industrial Airpark, a park-like setting featuring southwestern architecture .

From this location, Jack W. Fowler, president and chief executive officer, keeps in touch with the firm's six manufacturing centers and sales force through the use of the latest in data processing and communications systems. Krueger's individual printing centers offer a geographic network not often seen in the printing industry. The concept embodies a system of printing centers with complementing capabilities strategically located to satisfy customer distribution and production criteria. The six centers also have overlapping production capabilities which provide Krueger customers, who publish magazines, books, and catalogs, added backup assistance and flexibility for growth.

"Fifty years after Krueger began," comments president Fowler, "we can justifiably look back with pride, and we have in place the experience to look forward with anticipation."

W.A. Krueger corporate headquarters is located in a park-like setting in the Scottsdale Industrial Airpark, which during World War II was Thunderbird Field II, a 700-acre airfield where personnel were trained.

SALT RIVER PROJECT

Whether driving past posh country club resorts or window shopping in quaint specialty shops on Fifth Avenue, visitors and residents see Scottsdale as a city rich in style and charm. Scottsdale today, however, owes much of its refined character to early settlers who had a dream of taming the unpredictable Salt River which flows south of the city.

Those early settlers found the Salt River temperamental; sometimes it raged through the Valley and sometimes the river shrank to a trickle and crops withered and died. Consequently, many fled the Valley unable to cope with the whims of the river.

The Reclamation Act of 1902, signed by President Theodore Roosevelt, was the answer to their dilemma. The Act provided federal loans for construction of reclamation projects, including a dam for much-needed water storage.

A group of Valley pioneers then organized the Salt River Valley Water Users' Association, pledging their land as collateral on a loan to build what became the world's largest masonry dam serving landowners in a 250,000-acre service area. Thus Roosevelt Dam, located about 70 miles northeast of Scottsdale, was dedicated on March 18, 1911, six years after it was begun.

Since then a series of dams have been built along the Salt and Verde rivers, satisfying the Valley's need for a reliable water supply. Hydroelectric generating units on the dams along the Salt River also provide power necessary for a growing population.

Responsiblity for operation of the system belongs to the Salt River Valley Water Users' Association and the Salt River Project Agricultural Improvement and Power District, collectively known as the Salt River Project. The association and the district are independently governed by a publicly elected president, vice-president, board of directors, and council.

Among Scottsdale's early residents who served and are serving on the council are E.O. Brown, from 1910 to 1914 and again from 1922 to 1933; William L. Schrader, from 1956 to 1964 and his son, William P. Schrader, mayor of Scottsdale from 1962 to 1964, currently serving on the council; A. Warren Austin, from 1944 to 1948 and from 1960 to 1982; R.D. Searles, who was president from May 1948 to 1961; and George B. Willmoth, who was elected in 1956 and still serves.

SRP is the fifth-largest public power utility in the nation, providing electric power to 390,000 customers. With the Valley's rapid population growth, SRP has found additional power sources such as those that burn coal, oil, and natural gas. In recent years less than 12 percent of SRP's power has been hydroelectric. The majority has been generated by coal-fired stations.

Today the SRP provides water to customers in its service area with more than one million acre feet of water annually, almost enough to fill 23-mile-long Roosevelt Lake to capacity. The water is carried to municipal, agricultural, and industrial water users in Scottsdale and seven neighboring cities through an intricate 1,300-mile water delivery system.

Portions of two SRP canals that carry water wind through Scottsdale, providing recreation for joggers, bicyclists, equestrians, and fishermen. The Arizona Canal, built in 1883, passes through Scottsdale from the eastern city boundary at Pima Road to 64th Street. The new Crosscut Canal, built in 1912, runs parallel to 64th Street between the Arizona Canal at Indian School Road and the Grand Canal at Washington Street. The banks of the Crosscut contain the Valley's first concrete bicycle path, built in 1975.

Joggers and bicyclists enjoy recreation on the banks of the Arizona and new Crosscut canals in Scottsdale. The banks of the Salt River Project's canals were opened for recreation in 1964.

More than 1,500 of the Salt River Project's 5,000 employees work in the main administration building at Van Buren Street and Project Drive in Tempe.

ARIZONA PUBLIC SERVICE COMPANY

April 28, 1949, proved a landmark day for 375 Scottsdale customers of the Central Arizona Light and Power Company (Calapco). They became the city's first natural gas users, upon completion of a $90,000 gas pipeline project by the Arizona Public Service Company predecessor. A 7:45 p.m. twilight dedication ceremony counted Calapco executives and Scottsdale's Chamber of Commerce president among those in attendance, but the real stars of the show were gas lamps specially installed to demonstrate the new fuel's efficiency and economy.

It wasn't the first time Calapco had made a stir in Scottsdale. Ten years earlier the budding utility had completed a transmission line from Tempe and purchased area facilities from the Scottsdale Electric System, replacing the weaker 25-cycle power the city had formerly utilized from Salt River Valley Water Users' Association. The abundant and efficient new electrical service offered a myriad of possible uses to customers. Early consumer programs, including cooking classes for women, were offered by Calapco to help users learn how electricity could make their everyday lives easier.

As Scottsdale continued to grow at a phenomenal pace, so did the rest of Arizona, and it soon became apparent to utilities throughout the state that a more efficient way to meet customer needs was through a consolidated operation. In March 1952 Calapco merged with Arizona Edison to form Arizona Public Service Company. Nine months later a third utility, Northern Arizona Light and Power Co., joined the new venture, launching the organization that today reaches nearly 1,946,000 Arizonans, or about 70 percent of the state's population. More than 24,145 APS electrical users and 20,640 gas users are Scottsdale customers.

As the state's major utility, APS works continuously to meet Arizona's energy needs with the most economical and available generation fuels. From 1955 to 1960 the company built three gas-fired power plants—Saguaro, Yucca (jointly owned with Southern California Edison Co.), and Ocotillo. In the early 1960s APS pioneered the development of low-sulfur southwestern coal for power generation with the construction of the Cholla and Four Corners power plants in northeastern Arizona and New Mexico.

During the 1970s work was started on the expansion of Cholla and construction of Arizona's first nuclear power plant, the Palo Verde Nuclear Generating Station, currently nearing completion 55 miles west of Phoenix. The utility has also been involved with the development of solar power since 1955, when it helped found the Association for Applied Solar Energy, now known as the International Solar Energy Society. Today APS solar projects include a photovoltaic home in Yuma and a 225-kilowatt solar photovoltaic generating plant at Sky Harbor Airport.

Through the years Arizona Public Service has never lost sight of its most important goal: service to its customers. As the firm's standards of service and reliability continue, so will efforts to keep communities like Scottsdale living, working, and growing.

Careful placement of utility poles and lines helped preserve the Old West desert atmosphere that attracted thousands of yearly visitors to tourist shops such as these along Main Street in the early 1950s.

Knickers and broad-brimmed hats were the uniform of the day for gas crew members in 1930. Here one of the Valley's first gas lines is installed parallel to an unpaved street while supervisors look on.

TRANSCONTINENTAL PROPERTIES

What once was a quiet rolling desert where purebred Arabian horses and registered Angus cattle were bred and raised by Anne and Fowler McCormick has become one of the Southwest's most prestigious planned communities—McCormick Ranch—a 4,200-acre development that changed the course of Scottsdale's growth.

McCormick Ranch, noted for its land-use mix and amenities, which include a network of 11 lakes, 200 acres of open space and parks, and two championship 18-hole golf courses, has won acclaim as a model planned community from land developers and city planners throughout the nation. Local officials believe that the ranch is an example of what a master developer and a city can accomplish when they work in harmony toward mutual goals.

The development of McCormick Ranch commenced in July 1970 by Kaiser Aetna and resulted in the most intense land boom in Scottsdale's history. One of the development partners, Aetna Diversified Properties, took sole control of the development in 1977 and sold its assets to Transcontinental Properties in 1980.

The current master developer, Transcontinental Properties, is a partnership between Transcontinental Corporation of Santa Barbara, California, and the Bass family of Fort Worth, Texas. Its assets in addition to McCormick Ranch include 900 acres of industrial parks in Baltimore, Maryland, and Chicago, Illinois; a housing division, building 2,000 homes in a suburb of San Juan, Puerto Rico; and Gateway Plaza development in Steamboat Springs, Colorado. The other partnerships own a 1,000-acre business park, Harbor Bay Isle, along Alameda Bay in California; 800 acres in Ocean Pines, Maryland; and the 32,000-acre master planned Waikoloa Resort community in Hawaii.

The officers of Transcontinental Properties, who oversee the commercial development of the ranch and will be moving into a newly constructed corporate office building at 90th Street and Camelback Walk located in the 517-acre McCormick Ranch Center, are John E. Belda, president; Malcolm J. Bartlett, vice-president of development; Neal Burton, vice-president and treasurer; and William H. Paine, vice-president of acquisitions.

A thriving business and residential community with a projected population of 18,000 to 24,000, the ranch has three luxury resorts, The Registry, The Conference Center, and The Clarion Inn at McCormick Ranch; several condominium, town house, and apartment complexes and custom single-family residential homes ranging in price from $150,000 to $600,000; numerous garden-type office complexes and financial and banking institutions; a hospital; a post office; an elementary school; churches; a future city library; and four neighborhood shopping centers.

In addition, plans for McCormick Ranch Center, the business/commercial park east of Pima Road and south of Shea Boulevard, will include a 64-acre regional shopping center and resort hotel complex. The center also connects McCormick Ranch with the 1,119-acre Scottsdale Ranch at 96th Street, which was master-planned by Aetna and sold to Markland Properties in 1978.

In the future, Transcontinental plans to continue its development of prestigious industrial, commercial, and residential properties with an eye on southwestern regions of the United States while maintaining corporate headquarters on McCormick Ranch.

Once a working ranch where purebred Arabian horses and Angus cattle were bred, the McCormick Ranch development began in 1970. Under the guiding hand of Transcontinental Properties, the planned community has won nationwide acclaim for its land use.

PATRONS

The following individuals, companies, and organizations have made a valuable commitment to the quality of this publication. Windsor Publications and the Scottsdale Historical Society gratefully acknowledge their participation in *Scottsdale: Jewel in the Desert.*

Dale Anderson's Restaurants*
Arizona Conference of Seventh-day Adventists*
Arizona Public Service Company*
Wink Blair
Jorge A. Covarrubias, M.D.
Robert Davey Photography
El Chorro Lodge*
Est Est
Fowler Insurance Agency, Inc., est 1956
Walter L. Godber
Harris Trust Co.
The Impeccable Pig*
Iverson's Indian Arts and Crafts Studio*
Judson School*
W.A. Krueger Co.*
Russ Lyon Realty Company*
Lois and Loren McFarland
Markland Properties, Inc.*
Anna T. Martin
Messenger Mortuary & Chapel, Inc.*
William H. Messinger
Joe & Evie Miller
Motorola Inc.*
New Horizons Development Group, Ltd.
Paul's Hardware*
Gene Brown Pennington
The Ponderosa Lumber Co.*
Prestige Cleaners, Inc.
Quickcopy Printing Center/Donald F. & Nancy K. Smith
Mike Robbins
Rural/Metro Corporation*
Grover Ryan, Architect
Safari Resort*
Salt River Project*
Buck Saunders Trading Post and Gallery*
Vada Jean Thomas Scott
Scottsdale Board of REALTORS, Inc.*
Scottsdale Community College*
Scottsdale Memorial Hospital*
Scottsdale Plumbing Company, Inc.*
Sentry Insurance*
Gary Shapiro, Shapiro REALTORS
Charlie & Sally Smith
Sunflower Sandwich Shop Inc.
Transcontinental Properties*
Western Devcor Inc.*
Malcolm S. White
Donald M. Wiley
Carole and Chuck Zeman

*Partners in Progress of *Scottsdale: Jewel in the Desert.* The histories of these companies and organizations appear in Chapter 7, beginning on page 99.

SELECTED BIBLIOGRAPHY

BOOKS

Brandes, Ray. *Frontier Military Posts of Arizona.* Globe, Ariz.: Dale Stuart King, 1960.

Christensen, Ann; Lambert, Linda; and Sikes, Diane. *Phoenix: A Guide to Phoenix, Scottsdale and the Valley.* Phoenix: Valley Publishing Co., 1982.

Dick, Wilburn W. "The History of the Scottsdale School System at Scottsdale, Arizona, 1896-1944. Unpublished master's thesis, Arizona State Teachers College: 1944.

Everett, Ray. *Arizona History and Government.* Phoenix: Arizona State Board of Regents, 1977.

Faulk, Odie B. *Arizona, A Short History.* Norman: University of Oklahoma Press, 1970.

Fireman, Bert M. *Arizona, Historic Land.* New York: Alfred A. Knopf, 1982.

Gallegio, Hilario. "Reminiscences of an Arizona Pioneer." *Arizona Historical Review.* VI (Jan. 1935): 75-81.

Hayden, Carl T. *Charles Trumbull Hayden, Pioneer.* Tucson: Arizona Historical Society, 1972.

Lockwood, Frank C. *Pioneer Days in Arizona.* New York: The MacMillan Co., 1932.

Lynch, Richard E. *Winfield Scott, A Biography of Scottsdale's Founder.* City of Scottsdale, Ariz.: 1978.

Murphy, Merwin L. *W.J. and the Valley: The Story of W.J. Murphy and His Part in Developing the Salt River Valley in Arizona.* Alhambra, Calif.: Self-published, 1975.

Myrick, David F. *Railroads of Arizona.* Berkeley: Howell-North Books, 1975.

Pare, Madeline Ferrin, with the collaboration of Bert M. Fireman. *Arizona Pageantry.* Tempe: Arizona Historical Foundation, 1967.

Powell, Lawrence Clark. *Arizona, A Bicentennial History.* New York: W.W. Norton and Co.; Nashville: American Association for State and Local History, 1976.

Robinson, Dorothy F. *Arizona the Beautiful.* Scottsdale: Southwest Book Service, 1972.

Sacks, B. *Be It Enacted: The Creation of Arizona Territory.* Phoenix: Arizona Historical Foundation, 1964.

Salt River Project. *Taming of the Salt.* Phoenix: n.d.

Stevenson, Charles S. *We Met at Camelback.* Kingsport, Tenn.: Kingsport Press Inc., 1968.

Trimble, Marshall. *Arizona, A Panoramic View of a Frontier State.* Garden City, N.Y.: Doubleday and Co., Inc., 1977.

Wagoner, Jay J. *Arizona's Heritage.* Santa Barbara and Salt Lake City: Peregrine Smith, Inc., 1977.

Wagoner, Jay J. *Arizona Territory, 1863-1912, A Political History.* Tucson: University of Arizona Press, 1970.

Wyllys, Rufus K. *Arizona: The History of a Frontier State.* Phoenix: Hobson and Herr, 1950.

__________ . This Is Arizona, Arizona Republic, Phoenix: 1962.

__________ . Arizona. Sunset Discovery Books. Menlo Park, Calif.: Lane Book Co., 1963.

__________ . Alternate Futures for the City of Scottsdale. The Brookings Institution Seminars, 1971-72.

NEWSPAPERS AND MAGAZINES

Arizona Republican

Arizona Republic

Phoenix Gazette

Scottsdale Daily Progress

Scottsdale Quarterly

Scottsdale Scene

OTHER SOURCES

SPEECHES

"Scottsdale's Accomplishments and the Future."

Barr, Burton S. Sound recording, Mayor's Breakfast Series, May 26, 1981.

"Schools of Yesterday, Today and Tomorrow."

Reinholdt, Raymond. Sound recording, Mayor's Breakfast Series, October 23, 1980.

"Parada del Sol." Connelly, Lex. Sound recording, Mayor's Breakfast Series, January 29, 1981.

REPORTS

"Scottsdale 2,000: Direction for Tomorrow." STEP Committee's Interim Report to the City Council, June 1982.

Partners in Progress Index

Anderson's Restaurants, Dale, 101
Arizona Conference of Seventh-Day Adventists, 118
Arizona Public Service Company, 124
El Chorro Lodge, 111
Impeccable Pig, The, 106
Iverson's Indian Arts and Crafts Studio, 120
Judson School, 112
Krueger Co., W.A., 122
Lyon Realty Company, Russ, 108
Markland Properties, Inc., 121
Messenger Mortuary & Chapel, Inc., 103
Motorola Inc., 105
Paul's Hardware, 110
Ponderosa Lumber Co., The, 115
Rural/Metro Corporation, 113
Safari Resort, 109
Salt River Project, 123
Saunders Trading Post and Gallery, Buck, 114
Scottsdale Board of REALTORS, Inc., 102
Scottsdale Community College, 119
Scottsdale Historical Society, 100
Scottsdale Memorial Hospital, 107
Scottsdale Plumbing Company, Inc., 117
Sentry Insurance, 104
Transcontinental Properties, 125
Western Devcor Inc., 116

General Index

Italicized numbers indicate illustrations.

A
Adams, Bobbie, 78
Adobe House, The, 31, 85
Alberding, Charles, 64
All-Arabian Horse Show, 49, 78
Allison, Gordon, 68
All-Rite Cafe, 47
Ameche, Don, 50
American Legion Hall, 61, 69
Anderson, Dale, 66
Anti-Saloon League, 19
Apache Indians, 8, 19
Arabian Horse Association, 49
Arabian horses, 49, *59*
Arabian horse shows, *59*
Arcadia district, 29, 68
Arcadia High School, 65, 78
Arcosanti, 62
Arden, Elizabeth, 61
Arizona Bank, 55, 89, 99
Arizona Biltmore, 29, 41, 93
Arizona Canal, 15, 29, 31, 37, 44, 55, 58, 75, 92
Arizona Craft Center, 44, 53
Arizona Crafts building, 47
Arizona Craftsmen Council, 47, 48, 49, 57
Arizona Downs track, 42
Arizona Falls, 31
Arizona Falls generating plant, 36
Arizona Gazette, 23
Arizona Improvement Company, 13
Arizona Investment and Land Company, 21
Arizona Painters and Sculptors, 47
Arizona Public Service, 69
Arizona Republic, 43
Arizona Republican, 27, 39
Arizona Securities and Investment Company, 29
Arizona State University, 29, 52
Arizonian, 52, 74
Armour Research Center, 89
Art and Artists, 2, 25, *26*, 27, 44, *45*, *46*, 47-48, *49*, 52-53, 62, 81, *83*, *86-87*, *97*
Art Wagon, The, 81
Assembly of God members, 52
Austin, Warren, 55

B
Ball, Lucille, 50
Baltimore Orioles, 62, 64, 78, 79
Bank of Douglas, *54*, 55, 58
Bank of Scottsdale, 93
Baptist Hospital of Scottsdale, 79
Baptists, 34
Barclay, Don, 47
Barnes Butte, 8
Bartholow, Mildred, 31
Baseball, 37, 62, *63*, 64, 78, *79*, 93
Bashas' grocery store, 66
Basket House, 36
Bassham, Carl, *98*, 99
Bassham, Nina, *98*, 99
Bear Step, Shatka, *88*, 89
Beauchamp, Clara "Pansy" Boyer, 29, 78
Begay, Tony, 81
Benton, Patricia, 27, 61
Bimbo's Restaurant, 66
Blount, Alza, 16, 18, 19
Blount, George, 16, *17*, 18
Blount family, 21
Blue Socks, 37
Bonnell, Jon, 62
Boots and Saddles, 50
Borgata, The, 89, *94*
Boston Red Sox, 64
Boyd, James H., 52
Bratzel, Mildred K., 58
Briley, Charlie, 47
Brooks, Gabe, 37
Brown, Alvin, 34, *35*, *98*, 99
Brown, E.E. "Brownie," 55
Brown, Edwin O., *24*, 25, 32, 34, 36, 37, 47, 55, 59, 65
Brown, Ellsworth, 34, *35*, *98*, 99
Brown, Merle, 55
Brown, Ruth, *98*, 99
Brown, Shirley, 49
Brown, Suzanne, 81
Brown, Vergie Lutes, 58
Brown family, 25
Brown's general store, 29, 36, *38*, 39, 48
Buck Saunders Art Gallery, 53
Bunk House, The, 64
Burns, "Indian Tommy," 31
Byer's Market, 37
Byrnes, Ronald, *56*, 57
Byrnes, Sylvia, 50

C
Caldwell, Leona, 53
Camelback Inn, 42, *43*, 44, 62
Camelback Mountain, 8, 16, 29, *46*, 47, 62, 64, 68, 95, 99
Camelview Plaza, 89
Carefree, 48
Carefree Enterprise, 89
Carpenter, Cliff "Black Hat," 57
Casa Blanca Inn, 50, *51*
Casa Hermosa, 47
Cattle ranching, 32, 49, 65
Cavalliere, Mrs. Frank, 55
Cavalliere, George, *29*, 31, 58
Cavalliere, Mary Alice, 29
Cavalliere's blacksmith shop, *30*, 31, 58
Central Arizona Light and Power Company, 55, 57, 69
Central Arizona Project, 81
Chalee, Pop, 53
Chamber of Commerce, 96, 99
Chandler, 25, 36, 44, 62
Chaparral High School, 92
Cheney, Murle, 49
Chesnutt, Hunter, 32, *33*
Chew's grocery store, J., 36
Chez Louis, 68
Chicago Cubs, 78
Children's Fountain, The, *86*
China Lil's restaurant, 36
Christian Scientists, 69
Christine Rae's, 62
Citrus Homes Addition, 29
City Council, 61
City Hall, *59*, *77*, *83*, 92
City Hospital of Scottsdale, 79
Civic Center, 77, 83, 86
Civic Center Plaza, 97
Civil War, 15
Civitan Club, 65
Clayton, Bill, 71, *73*, 74, *75*
Coldwell, Adeline, *98*, 99
Coldwell, Charles, 36
Coldwell, Frank, *98*, 99
Coldwell, Lenore, *98*, 99
Coldwell, Tom, *98*, 99

Coldwell family, 25
Connolly, Francis, 52
Conrad, Glen, 47
Coronado High School, 32, 69, 71
Corporate Jets, 89
Corral, Emilio, 34
Corral, Jesus, 34, 61
Corral, Tomas, 31
Corral family, 41
Cosanti, 62
Cotton growing, 31
Coze, Paul, 61
Craft Center, 65
Craft Village, 53
Craig House, The, 62
Crews, Arthur, 32
Crews, Mrs. Arthur, *24*, 25
Crews, Grace, 48
Crews, Stanley, 48
Crews family, *24*, 25
Cronkite, Walter, 85
Crosier, Mildred, 68
Crosscut Canal, 41
Curtis, Philip, 44, *45*, 47
Cuthbert, Lucy, 31

D
Dairy farming, 31
Dalis, Nick, 64
Darlington, Tom, 48, *56*, 57
Davis, J.L., *18*, 25, 34
Davis, Lew, 44, *45*, 47, 48, 53
Davis family, 21
DeGrazia, Ted, 53
Depression, 39, 44, 52, 68
Der Steiner, 68
Desert Camp (D.C.) Ranch, 32
Desert Land Act of 1877, 13
Donaldson, Bill, 75
Douglas, James, 55
Drinkwater, Herb, *92*, 93
Dublin, "Buzz," 66, 67
Dublin, Mary Helen, 67
Dude ranches, 64
DuRoss, L.O., 32

E
Eagle and the Iron Cross, The, 52
Earl's Market, 37, 50, 58
Eckley's Soft Drink Emporium and Stage Office, 36
Edmiston, James G., 52
Education, 18, 27, *28*, 29, 32, *33*, 34, 42, 55, 65, 69, 71, 88, 92, *94*. *See also* Schools
Eisenhower, Mamie, 53, 85
Eitel, Mildred Sullivan, 7
El Chorro Lodge, 42, *43*, 50, 89
Eldorado Park, 79
Electronics industry, 65
Elliott, Judson A., 19
Elliott, Laura, *98*, 99
Elliott, Minnie, 19
Elliott, Myrtle, *98*, 99
Elliott, Polly, *98*, 99
Elliott family, 21
Elliott Sanatarium, 11
Ellis, Dora Jean, *28*, 29
Ellis, George, *40*, 41, 44
Episcopalians, 68
Erne, 53
Evans, Jessie Benton, 27, *31*
Evans, Robert, 31, 42, 50
Evans, Sylvia, 31
Executive House, 64

F
Falcon airfield, 48
Fannin, Paul, 71
Farmers' State Bank, 36, 39, 41, 65
Fashion Square, 58, 81
Ferber, Edna, 62
Festivals, *60*, 61, *90*
Fiesta Bowl, 64; marathon, 78
Fiorito, Ted, 50
Fire protection, 52, 58, *59*
First Baptist Church, 34, 66, 69
First Interstate Bank, 49
First National Bank, 37
Fleming, Irving, 88
Flying T Ranch, 64
Foehl, Robert, *56*, 57, 66
Foreman, Robert C., 79
Fort Huachuca, 15
Fort McDowell, 8
Fort McDowell Reservation, 37
Four Peaks, 9
Frederick, Jim, 66
Frederick, V.D., 58
Fredericks, Al, 31
Frederick's Auto and Livery Stable, 66
Fretz, George, 75, 85
Fulwiler, Nannie C. Utley, 15

G
Gabor, Zsa Zsa, 85
Gainey Ranch, 88
Gammill, Laurie, 23
Gammill, Maggie, 23
Gammill, Zona, 23
Garagiola, Joe, 78
Gardiner's Tennis Ranch, John, *95*
Gardner, Ava, 62
George, Roy, 37
Germaine, Louis, 68
Gleason, Jackie, 66
Glendale, 47, 48
Gluck, Etienne, 68
Goldwater, Barry, 42
Goldwaters Desert Fashions, 58
Gonzales, Bennie, *77*, 83, 86
Gorman, Alfred Kee, *80*, 81
Gorman, Carl N., *80*, 81
Gorman, Mrs. Carl N., *80*, 81
Gorman, R.C., *80*, 81
Gorman, Zonnie, *80*, 81
Graham, Emmette V., 50
Granite Reef Dam, 23
Graves, Edward "Buster," 25, *98*, 99
Graves, Mary Keene, 25, 34, *35*, 37, *98*, 99
Graves family, 25
Graves Guest Ranch, 25, 27, 96
Greene, Helen, *20*, 21
Griffith, Dick, 47
Gruber, Janet, 42
Gruber, Mark, 42, 50, 89

H
Handlebar J, 78
Hanny's, 58
Hanson, Eugene, 61
Harris, Phil, 66
Hashknife Gang, 61
Hayden, Ethel, 34, *35*
Hayden, Gussie, 34, *35*
Hayden, Helen, 34, *35*, *98*, 99
Hayden, Hugh, 34, *35*
Hayden, Mittie, 18, 34, *35*
Hayden, Wilford, 18, 32, 37
Hayden, Wilford "Boy," Jr., 34, *35*
Hayden Flour Mill, 8, 36
Health-seekers, 16, 18, 19, 21, 25, 27, 61-62
Herbergers, G. Robert, 64
Hermosa Inn, 47
Herrera, Barnebe, 31, 41
Herron and Walker Barbershop and Pool Hall, 36
Hilton Village, 89
Hobo Joe's, 55
Holbrook, 61
Hole-in-the-Rock, 21
Holmes, Nora, *98*, 99
Holveck, Thelma Steiner, 7, 23, *24*, 25, 39, 41
Hope, Bob, 85
Horwitch, Elaine, 81
Hospitals, 79, 92-93. *See also* individual hospitals
Hotel Adams, 47
Hotels, Inns, and Resorts, 25, *26*, 27, *30*, 31, 41, 42, *43*, 50, *51*, 64, *84*, 85, 88, 89, 93. *See also* individual hotels, inns, and resorts
House of Six Directions, 62
Howdy Dudettes, *72*, 73
Hubbell, Carl, 78
Huldermann, Paul, 62, 81
Humphrey, Hubert, 50, 64
Humphrey, Muriel, 64
Huntress, Jack, 66
Huon, Daniel, 68
Hydukovich, Joseph, 29

I

Incorporation, 55, 57
Indian Bend Slough, 23, 55
Indian Bend Wash, 75, 76, 77, 92; flood control project, 92; park system, 75
Indian Center, 55
Indian School Park, 92
Ingleside Inn, 25
Inn, The 88
Ireland, Imogene, 31

J
Jenkins, William, *89*, 92
Jennings, Waylon, 78
Johnson, Hoyt, 89
Jokake Inn, *30*, 31, 41, 50, 64, 66
Jokake School for Girls, 42
Judson, George, A. 42
Judson, Jeannette, 42
Judson School for Boys, 42

K
Kaiser Aetna, 85
KDOT radio, 74
Kelland, Clarence Buddington, 65
Kellogg, Donald, 50
Kerr, Louise Lincoln, 62
Kiami Lodge, 42
Kimsey, Clarice, 27
Kimsey, Elizabeth, 27, *28*, 29
Kimsey, Lois, 27
Kimsey, Mort, 27, 36, 37, *38*, 39, 57, 68, *69*, 71, 78
Kimsey, William E., 27, *28*, 29, 69
King, Thomas U.Z., 18
Kiva Craft Center, 34, 53
Kiva New, Lloyd, *48*, 53, 55, 62, 81
Kiva Theater, 55, 69
KOPA radio, 74
Kowal, Alexander, 53
Krueger Company, W.A., 89
KSGR radio, 74
Kubelsky, Lillian, 36
Kubelsky, Marshall, 36
Kubelsky-Boston Store, 36, 66
KWBY radio, 74

L
La Chaumiere, 68
La Merienda Cafe, 50
Lamfrom, Rudolph, 41
Last, Frank, 34, *35*
Last, Mrs. Frank, *98*, 99
Law, Bruce, 83
Le Bistro, 68
Le Coz, Pierre, 68
Lincoln, John C. 42
Lincoln Plaza, 89
Lindsey, Al, 41
Lindsey, Rosa, 41
Little Red Schoolhouse, 27, 29, 32, 61, 68, 69, 78, 97; Ball, 78
Loew's Paradise Valley Resort, 93
Loloma, Charles, 81
Loloma Elementary School, 32, 92. *See also* Scottsdale Grammar School
Lonewolf, Joseph, 81
Los Arcos Mall, 81
Los Olivos Restaurant, 97
Louise Lincoln Kerr Center, 62, *63*
Luce, Clare Boothe, 62
Lulu Belle's, 57, 66, 67
Lute's Pharmacy, 49, 58
Lynch, Richard, 9

M
McComb Brothers store, 36
McCormick, Fowler, 49
McCormick, Mrs. Fowler, 53
McCormick Ranch, 49, 50, *54*, 55, 85, 89; Inn, The, *84*, 85, 88
McCune, Walker, 68
MacDonald, Duncan, 42
McDowell Mountains, 9, 44, 99
McElfresh, Pat, 7
McGee's Indian Den, 58
Maes, Joseph, 53
Mag's Ham Bun Bunch, 58
Mag's restaurant, 61
Mahoney Mercantile, A.F., 36
Maine Chance, 53, 61
Malcolm, Richard, 74
Maricopa County, 57, 75
Maricopa Indians, 88
Marshall, Jonathan, 52, *74*, 96
Marshall, Thomas Riley, 27, 37
Marshall home, Thomas R., 68
Martin, Mary, 85
Masked Marvel, The, 31
Masonic Hall, 69
Mathis, May Vanderhoof, *96*, *98*, 99
Meadows, Bob, 62
Meadows, Margie, 62
Medicine Flower, Grace, 81
Megargee, Lon, 27, 44, 47
Mesa, 8, 15, 48, 79, 81
Messinger, Paul, 69
Messinger, Philip, 69
Messinger, William, 50, 58, 69
Messinger, William, Sr., 55
Messinger Mortuary, 69
Mesta, Perle, 62
Methodist Church, 41
Methodists, 34
Mexican Imports, 36
Mexican Revolution, 77
Miller, Bill, 57, 58
Miller, Charles, 23
Miller, Evie, 89
Miller, Joe, 50, 89
Miller, Murle, 32, *33*
Miller, William, 32, *33*, *98*, 99
Miracle of the Roses, The, 61
Moeur, B.B., 23, 39
Monday, Rick, 78
Morgan, Victor J., 52
Mormons, 8, 52
Motorola, Inc., 65
Mowry, Labeula Steiner, 7, 23, *24*, 25, 29, 39, 48
Mowry, Lester, 7, 29
Mummy Mountain, 9, 25, 42, *43*, 49, 99
Murdock, Rachel, 44
Murphy, William J., 13, 15, 21
Murray, Arthur, 66

N
National Bank of Scottsdale, 93
National Recovery Administration, 39
Neighborhood Development Program, 77
Nelson, Rick, 85
New, Lloyd Kiva, *48*, 53, 55, 62, 81
Newhart, Bob, 85
Newspapers and magazines, 37, 52, 74, 89. *See also* individual newspapers and magazines
Newton, Wayne, 85
Nevelson, Louise, 86
Nicklaus, Jack, 93
Noble, Daniel E., 65

O
Oakland Athletics, 78
Oasis Villa, 25
O'Brien, William, 62
O'Brien's Art Emporium, 62
Ogden, Claudia, 47
Old Maud, 16, *17*
Old Town, 29, 65, 97
One Civic Center Plaza, 97
Osborn School District, 42
Our Lady of Perpetual Help, 34, *35*, 58, 97

P
Paladin, David Chethlahe, 81
Palmer, Jim, 78, *79*
Palmer, K.T., 48
Papago Butte, 8
Papago Park, *20*, 21, 48, 52
Parada del Sol, *60*, 61, 88, 89, *91*, 93
Parades, *60*, 61, *91*, 93
Paradise Inn, 50, *51*, 57, 64
Paradise Park, 49
Paradise Valley, 85
Paradise Valley Guest Ranch, 64
Parks, 79, 92
Patio Book Shop, 50
Patio Fashions, 50
Patio Pantry, 50
Paul Shank's Fine Dining, 68
Paul's Hardware, 58
Pennington, Mrs. Gene Brown, 59
Peterson family, 25

Petley, Bob, 71
Pharmaceutical Card Systems, 89
Phoenician Resort Community, *95*
Phoenix, 6, 7, 8, 11, 13, 15, 18, 19, 21, 25, 27, 29, 34, 39, 41, 42, 47, 50, 52, 55, 57, 65, 68, 79, 81, 85, 93, 97
Phoenix Herald, The, 16, 19
Picket Fence, 50
Pickford, Mary, 62, 85
Pima Indians, 15, 19, 21, 37, 88
Pima Plaza, 37
Pink Pony, 47
Police-City Court Complex, 77
Porter's Western Wear, 37, *38,* 39, 52, 55, 58, 62
Portofino Theater, 50
Posie Post, 65
Powder Horn Ranch, 37
Presbyterians, 34
Prescott, 18, 31
Prohibition, 39
Pruitt, Hurley, 58

R
Radio stations, 74
Radisson Resort, 50
Rancher, The, 89
Ranchera Fashions, 50
Ranch House, 66
Rancho Vista Bonita, 64
Rangel family, 41
Read, Avis, 44
Reagan, Michael, 42
Reagan, Ronald, 42
Recreation, 37, *38,* 39, 42, 78, *95*
Red Dog Saloon, 79
Redstar, Kevin, 81
Registry Resort, The, 88
Religion, 19, 34, *35,* 52, 68-69
Restaurants, 29, 31, 36, 47, 50, 58, 66, 67, 68. *See also* individual restaurants
Ride 'n' Rock Ranch, 50
Rinehart, Bob, 89
Rinehart, Marge, 89
Roosevelt, Anna, 64
Roosevelt, Eleanor, 53, 64
Roosevelt Dam, 23
Rose, Johnny, 34
Rose's Pool Hall, Johnny, 36, 97
Royal Palms Inn, 50, 64
Rubenstein, "Popcorn John," 21
Rural-Metro Fire Department, 52, 58, *59*
Rusty Spur, The, 65
Ryan, Pat, 64

S
Saba, David, Jr., 62
Saba, Edward, 62
Saba, Norman, 62
Saba, Richard, 62
Saba, Roger, 62
Saba's Department Store, 37, 58, 62
Safari Hotel and Resort, 64, 68
Saguaro Bar, 57, 66
Saguaro High School, 71
St. Louis Writers Plantation Club, 25
Sakowitz Store, 89
Salt River, 6, 23, 27, 75
Salt River Pima-Maricopa Indian Community, 85, 88
Salt River Valley, 7, 13, 23, 99
Salt River Valley Water Users Association, 23
Sampair, Pat, 79
San Carlos Hotel, 29
Sanderson, Phillips, *46,* 47
San Francisco Giants, 78
San Marcos Hotel, 25
Santa Fe Railroad, 8
Saunders, Buck, 52, 53, 62
Scandinavian, 81
Schaefer, Mathilde, 44, 47, 53
Schimmel, William, 53
Schneider, Philip H., 57
Scholder, Fritz, 81
School District 48, 18
Schools: Arcadia High, 65, 78; Chaparral High, 92; Coronado High, 32, 69, 71; Jokake School for Girls, 42; Judson School for Boys, 42; Loloma Elementary, 32, 92; Saguaro High, 71, 1896 School, 18; Scottsdale Grammar, 32, 34, 65; Scottsdale High, 32, 48, 52, 65, 66, 68, 78, 79, 94; Tempe Normal, 8; Winfield Scott Junior High, 55
Schrader, Bill, 71, *72,* 73
Schrader, William, Sr., 47
Scott, Elliott "Scotty," 37, 58
Scott, George Washington, *15*
Scott, Helen Louise Brown, *14,* 15, 16, *17, 20,* 21, 27, 34
Scott, Winfield, 8, 13, *14,* 15, 16, *20,* 21, 27, 34, 66, *83,* 92, 93, 96, 97, 99; home of, 66
Scottsdale Booster, 52
Scottsdale Boys Club, 65
Scottsdale Bulletin, 37
Scottsdale Cafe, 29
Scottsdale Camelback Hospital, 93
Scottsdale Center for the Arts, 77, *82,* 83, 90, 97
Scottsdale Chamber of Commerce, 34, 41, 52, 78
Scottsdale Charros, 78
Scottsdale Commercial Bank, 93
Scottsdale Community College, 88
Scottsdale Community Hospital, 92
Scottsdale Community Players, 61
Scottsdale Conference Center, 88
Scottsdale Coordinating Committee, 65
Scottsdale Daily Progress, 32, 52, 53, 74, 78, 96
Scottsdale Financial Center, 96
Scottsdale Ginning Company, 36
Scottsdale Girls Club, 65
Scottsdale Grammar School, 32, 34, 65. *See also* Loloma Elementary School
Scottsdale Hardware, 58
Scottsdale High School, 32, 48, 52, 65, 66, 68, 78, 79, 94; Beaver Band, 61; Old Main, *94*
Scottsdale Historical Society, 78, 89, 92
Scottsdale Industrial Air Park, 81
Scottsdale Jaycees, 61
Scottsdale Journal, 52
Scottsdale Light and Power Company, 27, 36
Scottsdale Mall, 34, 77
Scottsdale Memorial Hospital, *70,* 71, 79, 92
Scottsdale Memorial Hospital North, 92
Scottsdale Methodist Church, 34
Scottsdale Motors, 58
Scottsdale Municipal Airport, *80,* 81
Scottsdale National Indian Arts Exhibition, 81
Scottsdale Pharmacy, 36, 49
Scottsdale Presbyterian Church, 69, 76
Scottsdale Quarterly, 89
Scottsdale Scene, 89
Scottsdale Service Company, 27, 37, 58
Scottsdale Symphony Orchestra, 34, 88
Scottsdale Towers Hotel, 89
Scottsdale Town Enrichment Program (STEP), 74, 75, 77, 89, 92
Scottsdale United Cable, 89, 92
Scottsdale YMCA, 44
Scotty's Blacksmith Shop, 58, 66
Security Acres, plat of, *28,* 29
Segner, Wes, 48, *49,* 52, 53
Seidel, Lottie, 50
Sentry Insurance, 89
Serviss, George "Bud," *98,* 99
Settlers, first, 16-21
Seventh-Day Adventist Conference, 81
Sewell, Brice, 62
Sewell, Judy, 62
Shank, Paul, 68
Shipp, Earl, 7, 37, 49, *60,* 61
Shoeman, John, 58
Shutters, The, 68
Sky Harbor Airport, 29, 50
Sloan, Richard, 27
Smith, Walter P., *20,* 21, 37
Smith, Mrs. Walter P., *98,* 99
Smothers, Tommy, 85
Snowball, 42, *43*
Soleri, Paolo, 62
Song, Jackson, 36
Song, Jew Chew, 36
Song, John, 36
Southern Baptist Convention, 79
Southside Progress, 52
Southwest Studies Institute, 88

Sparks, Flo, 65
Sparks, "Sparky," 65
Spielberg, Steven, 78
Stable Gallery, 44
Stagebrush Theater, 61
Steiner, Jacob, 23, *24,* 25
Steiner, Labeula. *See* Mowry, Labeula Steiner
Steiner, Lorene, 23, *24,* 25
Steiner, Thelma. *See* Holveck, Thelma Steiner
Steiner family, 41
Sterling Drug, 36
Steven Restaurant, 78
Stewart, Jack, 42, 64
Stewart, Louise, 42
Stillman, Guy, 68
Stone, Steve, 78
Strobel, Oscar, Jr., 27, 47
Sugar Bowl, The, 66
Sullivan, Oscar, 41
Sundial Guest Ranch, 64
Sun Down Ranch, 64
Sunshine Festival, 61
Sun Valley Pool, 52
Superstition Mountains, 9
Sussman, Ruth, 62
Swarthout, Glendon, 52
Swick, Andy, 55
Swick, Harriet, 55
Swick's Clothing Store, 55, 58
Sweeney, Jack, 58

T
Tait, John S., 18
Taliesin West, 44, *45, 87*
T-Bar-T Theater, 55, 57, 69
Tempe, 6, 8, 15, 19, 34, 36, 49, 52, 57, 81, 85
Tempe Daily News, 52
Tempe Normal School, 8
Temperance, 19
Tent-houses, 19
Thies, Al, 66
Thomas, George, 21, 34, *35,* 57, 65, *98,* 99
Thomas, George, Jr., 48
Thomas, Grace, 32, *98,* 99
Thomas, Marjorie, 2, 25, *26,* 27, *97*
Thomas, Sarah, 21
Thomas, Stanley Ellis, 21, 34, *35, 98,* 99
Thomas family, 25
Thunderbird I Airfield, 48, 81
Thunderbird II Airfield, 48
Tico Taco Mexican Restaurant, 58
Tims, B.L. "Bud," *75,* 92
Titus, Frank F., 18
Titus House, 16, *17,* 18
Trader Vic's, 68
Trading Post, The, 52
Travis family, 64
Tres Jolie, 50
Trimble, Ira "Happy," 6
Trimble, Marshall, 7
Trumbull, Rose, *26,* 27
Tucson, 13, 81
Turquoise Ranch, 64

U
Underhill, Howard, 19, *20,* 21
Underhill, Ida, 19, *20,* 21
Underhill family, 21
Underhill home, 21
Utley, Albert G., 15, 16, 19
Utley, Margaret Murphy Leander, 15

V
Valley Ho Hotel, 64, 66
Valley National Bank, 78
Vanderhoof, James, 34, *35, 98,* 99
Vanderhoof, Jane P., 27
Vanderhoof, Perla "May," 18, *20,* 21, 34, *35, 98,* 99
Vanderhoof, Verner A., 18,*20,* 21, 34
Verde River Water Project, 44
Village Patio, 50
Vista del Camino, 77, 88

W
Wagner, Robert, 66
Walthall, Anna Mae, 25
Walthall, Henry, 25
Ward, Frances, 34, *35*
Wasbotten, Luther "Lute," 49, *60,* 61
Wayne, John, 50, 85
Western Savings and Loan, 66
Westward Ho, 41
White, Garland, 32
White, Malcolm, 47, 55, 57, *58,* 65, 68, 93
White, Mary Brown, 15
White Hogan, 62
Whitey's Cafe and Bar, 47
Wick, Henry C., III, *42,* 48
Wigwam Department Store, 91
Wigwam Resort, 41, 42, 66
Wild Bill's, 78
Williams, John Elmer, *98,* 99
Williams Airfield, 48
Williams Air Force Base, 61
Willmoth, Gwendolyn, *46,* 47
Willmoth, J.T., 39
Willmoth, Norma, *46,* 47
Willmoth, Ruby, 47
Willmoth, Tom, 47
Willmoth Appliance, 58
Winchell, Walter, 50
Windows to the West, 86
Winfield Scott Junior High School, 55
Witzeman, Lou, 52, 58, 59
Wong, Joe, 65
Wood, Natalie, 66
Woolworth Company, F.W., 66
Works Projects Administration, 41
World War I, 31
World War II, 48
Woudenberg, John, 71, *72,* 73
Wright, Frank Lloyd, 44, 62, 87, 93
Wright, Olgivanna, 44
Wrigley Mansion, 29
Writers, 25, *26,* 27

Y
Yaqui Indians, 32, 77
Yellow Boot Ranch, 64
Yuschik, Leonard, 48

Z
Zaharek, Val, 53

A diversion around the turn of the century was a trip to the Arizona Falls, near the present Indian School Road and 56th Street. The Arizona Canal had been channeled over a rock shelf, creating a 16-foot cascade. In later years a dance pavilion was built that provided additional attraction on desert evenings. Later, the falls provided the area with its first electricity. Courtesy, Mrs. Jane Murphy McDaniel

Books in the Windsor History Series

ALABAMA
The Valley and the Hills: An Illustrated History of Birmingham and Jefferson County, by Leah Rawls Atkins
Historic Huntsville: City of New Beginnings, by Elise Hopkins Stephens
Mobile: The Life and Times of a Great Southern City, by Melton McLaurin and Michael Thomason
Montgomery: An Illustrated History, by Wayne Flynt

ARIZONA
Scottsdale: Jewel in the Desert, by Patricia Myers McElfresh
Tucson: Portrait of a Desert Pueblo, by John Bret Harte

CALIFORNIA
Heart Of The Golden Empire: An Illustrated History of Bakersfield, by Richard C. Bailey
California Wings: A History of Aviation in the Golden State, by William Schoneberger
Los Angeles: A City Apart, by David L. Clark
Sacramento: Heart of the Golden State, by Joseph A. McGowan & Terry R. Willis *San Bernardino County: Land of Contrasts,* by Walter C. Schuiling
International Port Of Call: An Illustrated Maritime History of the Golden Gate, by Robert J. Schwendinger
Stockton: Sunrise Port on the San Joaquin, by Olive Davis

COLORADO
Life In The Altitudes: An Illustrated History of Colorado Springs, by Nancy E. Loe
Denver: America's Mile High Center of Enterprise, by Jerry Richmond

CONNECTICUT
We Crown Them All: An Illustrated History of Danbury, by William E. Devlin
Hartford: An Illustrated History of Connecticut's Capital, by Glenn Weaver
New Haven: An Illustrated History, edited by Floyd Shumway and Richard Hegel
Stamford: An Illustrated History, by Estelle F. Feinstein, & Joyce S. Pendery

FLORIDA
Fort Lauderdale & Broward County: An Illustrated History, by Stuart McIver

IDAHO
Boise: An Illustrated History by Merle Wells

ILLINOIS
Chicago: Commercial Center of the Continent, by Kenan Heise and Michael Edgerton
Des Plaines: Born of the Tall Grass Prairie, by Donald S. Johnson
Prairie of Promise: Springfield and Sangamon County, by Edward J. Russo

INDIANA
The Story of Evansville, by Kenneth P. McCutchan
The Fort Wayne Story: A Pictorial History, by John Ankenbruck
Muncie And Delaware County: An Illustrated Retrospective, by Wiley W. Spurgeon, Jr.
Terre Haute: Wabash River City, by Dorothy J. Clark

IOWA
Cedar Rapids: Tall Corn and High Technology, by Ernie Danek

LOUISIANA
River Capital: An Illustrated History of Baton Rouge, by Mark T. Carleton
New Orleans: An Illustrated History, by John R. Kemp

MARYLAND
Baltimore: An Illustrated History, by Suzanne Ellery Greene
Montgomery County: Two Centuries of Change by Jane C. Sween

MASSACHUSETTS
Boston: City on a Hill, by Andrew Buni & Alan Rogers
The Valley and its Peoples: An Illustrated History of the Lower Merrimack River, by Bul Hudon
Heart of the Commonwealth: Worcester, by Margaret A. Erskine

MICHIGAN
Battle Creek: The Place Behind the Products, by Larry B. Massie, & Peter J. Schmitt
Jackson: An Illustrated History, by Brian Deming
Kalamazoo: The Place Behind the Products, by Peter J. Schmitt & Larry B. Massie
Out of a Wilderness: An Illustrated History of Greater Lansing, by Justin L. Kestenbaum
Saginaw: A History of the Land and the City, by Stuart D. Gross

MINNESOTA
Duluth: An Illustrated History of the Zenith City, by Glenn N. Sandvik
City of Lakes: An Illustrated History of Minneapolis, by Joseph Stipanovich
Saint Cloud: The Triplet City, by John J. Dominick
St. Paul: Saga of an American City, by Virginia Brainard Kunz

MISSOURI
From Southern Village to Midwestern City: Columbia, An Illustrated History, by Alan R. Havig
At the River's Bend: An Illustrated History of Kansas City, Independence and Jackson County, By Sherry Lamb Schirmer & Richard D. McKinzie
Springfield of the Ozarks, by Harris and Phyllis Dark

MONTANA
Montana: Land of Contrast, by Harry W. Fritz

NEBRASKA
Lincoln: The Prairie Capital, by James L. McKee
Omaha and Douglas County: A Panoramic History, by Dorothy Devereux Dustin

NEVADA
Reno: Hub of the Washoe County, An Illustrated History, by William D. Rowley

NEW HAMPSHIRE
New Hampshire: An Illustrated History of the Granite State, by Ronald & Grace Jager

NEW JERSEY
Morris County: The Progress of its Legend, by Dorianne R. Perrucci
A Capital Place: The Story of Trenton, by Mary Alice Quigley and David E. Collier

NEW YORK
Albany: Capital City on the Hudson by John J. McEneny
Broome County Heritage: An Illustrated History, by Lawrence Rothwell
Buffalo: Lake City in Niagara Land, by Richard C. Brown and Bob Watson
Harbor & Haven: An Illustrated History of the Port of New York, by John G. Bunker
A Pictorial History of Jamestown & Chautauqua County, by B. Dolores Thompson
The Upper Mohawk Country: An Illustrated History of Greater Utica, by David M. Ellis

A Panoramic History of Rochester and Monroe County, New York, by Blake McKelvey
Syracuse: From Salt to Satellite, by Henry W. Schramm and William F. Roseboom

NORTH CAROLINA
Greensboro: A Chosen Center, by Gayle Hicks Fripp
Raleigh: City of Oaks, by James E. Vickers
Cape Fear Adventure: An Illustrated History of Wilmington, by Diane Cobb Cashman

OHIO
Butler County: An Illustrated History, by George C. Crout

OKLAHOMA
Heart of the Promised Land: An Illustrated History of Oklahoma County, by Bob L. Blackburn

PENNSYLVANIA
Allegheny Passage: An Illustrated History of Blair County, by Robert L. Emerson
Erie: Chronicle of a Great Lakes City, by Edward Wellejus
An Illustrated History of Greater Harrisburg, by Michael Barton
The Heritage of Lancaster, by John Ward Willson Loose
The Lehigh Valley: An Illustrated History, by Karyl Lee Hall and Peter Hall
Williamsport: Frontier Village to Regional Center, by Robert H. Larson, Richard J. Morris, and John F. Piper, Jr.
The Wyoming Valley: An American Portrait, by Edward F. Hanlon
To the Setting of the Sun: The Story of York, by George R. Sheets

RHODE ISLAND
Rhode Island: The Independent State, by George H. Kellner and J. Stanley Lemons

SOUTH CAROLINA
Charleston: Crossroads of History, by Isabella G. Leland
Columbia, South Carolina: History of a City, by John A. Montgomery

TENNESSEE
Chattanooga: An Illustrated History, by James Livingood
Metropolis of the American Nile: An Illustrated History of Memphis and Shelby County, by John E. Harkins

TEXAS
Beaumont: A Chronicle of Promise, by Judith Linsley & Ellen Rienstra
Corpus Christi: The History of a Texas Seaport, by Bill Walraven
Dallas: An Illustrated History, by Darwin Payne
City at the Pass: An Illustrated History of El Paso, by Leon Metz
Houston: Chronicle of the Supercity on Buffalo Bayou, by Stanley E. Siegel
Waco: Texas Crossroads, by Patricia Ward Wallace

UTAH
Salt Lake City: The Gathering Place, by John S. McCormick

VIRGINIA
Norfolk's Waters: An Illustrated Maritime History of Hampton Roads, by William Tazewell

WASHINGTON
King County And Its Queen City: Seattle by James Warren
South On The Sound: An Illustrated History of Tacoma & Pierce County, by Rosa & Murray Morgan

WEST VIRGINIA
Charleston and the Kanawha Valley: An Illustrated History, by Otis K. Rice
Wheeling: An Illustrated History, by Doug Fetherling

WISCONSIN
Follow The Fox: An Illustrated History of the Fox River Valley, by Ellen Kort
Green Bay: Gateway to the Great Waterway, by Betsy Foley

CANADA
Calgary: Canada's Frontier Metropolis, by Max Foran & Heather McEwan Foran
Edmonton: Gateway to the North, by John F. Gilpin
Hamilton: Chronicle of a City, by T. Melville Bailey
Kitchener: Yesterday Revisited, by Bill Moyer
Where Rivers Meet: An Illustrated History of Ottawa, by Courtney C. J. Bond
Regina: From Pile O'Bones to Queen City of the Plains, by W.A. Riddell
Saint John: Two Hundred Years Proud, by George W. Schuyler
Saskatoon: Hub City of the West, by Gail A. McConnell
Toronto: The Place of Meeting, by Frederick H. Armstrong
Winnipeg: Where the New West Begins, by Eric Wells by Bill Moyer

THIS BOOK WAS SET IN

PALATINO TYPE

PRINTED ON

70-POUND ACID-FREE MEAD

AND BOUND BY

WALSWORTH PUBLISHING
COMPANY